THE UNIVERSITY IN A CHANGING WORLD

A SYMPOSIUM

Edited by
WALTER M. KOTSCHNIG
AND ELINED PRYS

Essay Index Reprint Series

 BOOKS FOR LIBRARIES PRESS
FREEPORT, NEW YORK

First Published 1932
Reprinted 1969

STANDARD BOOK NUMBER:
8369-1183-0

LIBRARY OF CONGRESS CATALOG CARD NUMBER:
71-86766

PRINTED IN THE UNITED STATES OF AMERICA

CONTENTS

Introduction

By WALTER M. KOTSCHNIG

IT is the need of the younger generation in the universities, of the generation 'between the ages', which has led to the publication of this book. It has grown out of the suffering of those who in 1919 came back from the trenches to fight for a new ideal of humanity and were defeated; and of those who are students to-day and have never known anything but a world in chaos. Many of them have met in the international conferences of *International Student Service*. In the beginning, when *International Student Service* was still called *European Student Relief*, they met simply to discuss ways and means of relieving the physical suffering of post-War students. Soon, however, other considerations broke through. It became clear that the moral and intellectual need in the student world was as great as the purely physical penury, moreover that it was not confined to those countries upon which the disastrous consequences of the War were telling most heavily. Numerous discussions on 'university ideals' followed, and in 1925 a publication[1] appeared which reported some of the addresses and statements made in these discussions. It was the first effort after the War to bring out the underlying tendencies and ideas which universities of all countries had in common, and to give a stable basis to international university collaboration, equally far removed from the vaporous

---

[1] *Die Universitätsideale der Kulturvölker*, edited by Reinhold Schairer and Conrad Hoffmann, Jr.; Quelle & Meyer, Leipzig, 1925.

ideas of a sentimental pacifism and from the slogans of an overheated nationalism. As a first effort it was remarkable, but the circumstances under which the statements were made —the troubled atmosphere of one of the early international student conferences after the War—rendered their value somewhat problematic. Only a few of them penetrated to really fundamental issues.

Whatever the defects of this first publication, it served to stimulate further discussion. Increasing emphasis was laid on bringing together professors and students of different countries to try to bridge the gulf which the War had opened between them. Specific problems of the modern universities were raised and investigated. Their overcrowding, their adjustment to new economic social conditions, the problems of vocational guidance and of selection were one by one considered. As the study of these problems progressed the need for a comprehensive inquiry into the various university systems and into the ideas behind them became more and more evident. Even problems which seemed, to begin with, purely organizational and technical led to the crucial question: what is the purpose of the university, and how can it be met? To quote only one example, no adequate selection of students is possible so long as there is no standard of values by which to judge them, and that standard of values can only be established in so far as there is a common idea of the nature of the institution for which they are to be selected. It is significant of the lack of a common idea of higher learning that the tests and standards applied for selection in countries like France, Germany, and the United States differ considerably from each other, and that, moreover, in every one of these countries voices are raised in protest against the means of selection in use. From the study of the concrete problems of the universities and of the general situation in which they find themselves on the one hand, and from the uneasiness and unrest of all serious students within them on the other, has come the need for a comprehensive study of the conception or conceptions of the university.

In a period which has shelved philosophy, which owns no philosophical idea or system of ideas of world-wide validity, which has not produced a genius whose thought can answer the anxious questions of a chaotic world, it would have been impossible to produce a synthesis of all present conceptions of the university, and extremely difficult even to make an unbiased statement of their conflicting bases. Our study of the various systems has therefore taken the form of a symposium, in which outstanding representatives of the various countries present a picture of their respective universities, the ideas that dominate within them, their methods and the concepts they embody.

The selection of the university systems treated in this book needs no explanation. They are those which have the largest numbers of students, and which have most profoundly influenced the organization and character of higher education in the rest of the world. An article on the Catholic idea of the university has been included, not only because that idea played a great role in the formation of the earlier universities, but also because it has been gaining ground again recently and has contributed a most constructive line of thought to the general discussion of this important subject. The editors originally intended to include further articles on Spain and the Far East—Spain, because the development of its universities and the place they have taken in the life of the nation in recent times is typical of much that is happening in all the Spanish-speaking countries in the New World as well as the Old; and the Far East, because of the vitally significant tendencies both in India and China towards emancipation of the universities from the western ideas which have dominated them hitherto. Space has made such an extension of the book impossible, but it is to be hoped that at a later stage it will be possible to make up for these omissions.

The Constituent Elements of the University

The character of a university is determined by the idea of knowledge which it professes to advance, by the type of man it purports to produce, and by the economic, social, and political condition of the community in which it finds itself.

Let us examine first the idea of knowledge. In so far as there is or has been one idea of knowledge, one conception of truth transcending all the differences in constitution developed by individual universities, in so far can we speak of *the* university, guardian of the *summum bonum* of man's intellectual achievement.

The idea of this university exists at present only as a memory of past greatness or as a hope for the future. The oneness of learning which once united all the universities, irrespective of their differences, has broken down. Their conception of truth, their methods, the way they conceive their purpose vary from country to country. Whereas formerly they believed that in them was vested the absolute, or as much of it as the human mind could perceive, they now appear to be altogether too much conditioned by their differing environments. Let there be no mistake—the agglomerate of facts which is the common possession of all institutions of learning, scientific inventions which become universal property as soon as they are made, are not an equivalent for that lost unity of truth and learning. Facts, in a world of economic values, may become significant in so far as they are put to useful purposes, but they are without fundamental meaning as long as they are not related to a higher principle with which they can be co-ordinated and by which—within limits—they can be explained. The history of the universities is ideally the history of man's search after that principle.

There have been periods in this history when man believed that the all-embracing principle had been discovered, that truth had been found. Each of these periods represented a climax, not only in the development of the human mind but also in the power, the position, and the influence of the universities.

In their early beginnings it was the conception of the *unitas intellectus* of Thomas Aquinas, in which faith and knowledge became one, which gave them their superiority over the temporal powers and made them centres both of religion and of intellectual achievement. The university found its deepest oneness in the oneness of God. Then Humanism turned from God to Man, from the contemplation of heaven to the exploration of earth, without severing the connexion between the two. In conceiving man as a microcosm, it understood the world as a macrocosm.

The period of Enlightenment established the goddess of reason as arbiter of truth and falsehood. It conceived the world as essentially built on reason. In reason it found both the unity of the world and the way to understand it. In the beginning it gave new lustre to the universities; but it prepared the way for their downfall. 'Reason' was soon replaced by her twin-sister 'utility'. Utility in turn led to the subordination of the universities to 'reasons of State' and to other ends unconnected with their fundamental task as it had been first understood, the discovery and contemplation of truth. In the last few decades of the eighteenth century, very much as at present, we find an abundance of proposals to replace the universities altogether by professional and technical schools.

With the Romantic period, however, a reaction set in, particularly in Germany, which led to a revival. Romanticism evolved an idea of the world in which its unity was discovered anew, in which the contrast between nature and the human mind disappeared. In the realm of pure thought, said the Romantics, subject and object are identical, nature and history become one. 'Pure thought (*Wissenschaft*) is the annihilation of the contrast, the reunion of the originally united', says Steffen in his *Grundzüge der philosophischen Naturwissenschaft*. Philosophy has never recovered the high esteem in which it was then held as the alpha and omega of the true university.

The dialectics of historical development led to the period of Auguste Comte and his Positivism. Philosophy had to cede the supreme place to the natural sciences and their methods. The new possession which all the universities in all their faculties have in common is the scientific method. From a new standpoint it seems true that there is no real difference between matter and man. Man is matter, and as such can be explored by the same methods as are used in the natural sciences. All standards of values are to be banned from the university. At last things are to be seen as they are; 'science without presuppositions' (*voraussetzungslose Wissenschaft*) is born. Real knowledge is obtained at last, and this means power—power over the world, whose secrets are at last being discovered. Far removed as we may be to-day from this conception of knowledge, there can be no doubt that it constituted the last period of real greatness which our universities have seen. It carried with it the claim of the absolute. While the universities did not pretend to know everything, they were certain that progress achieved by the methods common to all of them would lead them to final truth. It was still possible to speak of *the* university.

Nietzsche was amongst the first to shatter this myth; for Bergson's 'intuition' there was no place in the old system. Even so their vitalistic philosophies might have led to a fresh search for essential truth, had it not been for the breaking in of elements which were entirely strange to that purpose. What Napoleon had failed to create, the Babbitt of all lands attempted with more success—a university to produce good citizens, not inspired by the heroic ethics of Fichte and his metaphysics of the nation-state, but loyal to the régime of the day. This new university was to furnish the world with good doctors and lawyers and chemists, for Mr. Babbitt needed them for his comfort. It was to produce students pledged to the various party programmes, for in them was truth. The amorality of the positivist period was replaced by the immorality which declares all values to be relative— and Einstein, one of the few heroes of the mind who was left, was quoted as a witness. Thomas Aquinas was relegated to the attic with his *magna charta* of the university, which, to him was the embodiment of man's speculative mind: 'Intellectus speculativus est qui, quod apprehendit non ordinat ad opus, sed ad solam veritatis considerationem.'[1]

We have come, though by no dignified road, to the second of our determining factors in the character of the university, viz. the kind of individual it aims at producing.

The universities of all ages professed not only to advance knowledge but to produce an *élite* in thought and leadership. In every period this *élite* was formed under the influence of the prevailing idea of learning and the corresponding ideal of man. The Middle Ages knew the scholar-saint, humanism with its Greek traditions the sage, romanticism had its own concept of 'the scholar and ethical personality', and positivism proclaimed its idea of leadership in the words 'knowledge is power'. These images were naturally modified from country to country by the national genius. The rise of national self-consciousness emphasized these modifications, but did not disrupt beyond repair the unified ideal of man.

To-day there is no common idea of the *élite*, any more than there is a common idea of truth and learning. There are,

[1] Dr. Doerne in his article on the German universities analyses in great detail the elements in positivism itself which led to this development.

as we shall see, countries like Italy which are not troubled by any doubts as to the justification of their ideal of learning, and in these countries there exists a corresponding conception of the kind of man the universities should produce. In other countries, like Germany, where both within and without the universities the 'crisis of learning' is proclaimed, cries of warning are being raised on every hand because the universities 'fail to bring forth an *élite*'. And this in spite of the fact that Germany has a national system of training and selection, ensuring, by a wise and elaborate scheme of scholarships and other aids, that higher education shall be open to the highly gifted in all classes of the population.

Most significant of all are the many voices denouncing what has been called *La trahison des clercs*.[1] University men, the medieval *clerici*, whose privilege it has been to inherit the sum of the race's knowledge and to whom has been vouchsafed the inspiration of national, cultural, and spiritual tradition, have abandoned the cause of truth and justice, which they were called upon to serve. Trained as they were, partially at least, at the expense of the nation, they have sold their ability, their skill, and knowledge to the forces of self-interest which dominate the world to-day and block the way to a fuller, wider, and freer life. Greed, the will to power, desire for security and comfort have betrayed those trained to be the *élite* into committing this worst of all treasons. And men begin to ask: Is not the present university responsible for this diversion of talent to base ends? Does it not actually incite to this grand betrayal of the intellectuals by attempting to give a theoretical justification of our present society, and by training men who will serve this present order willingly, asking no questions?

We are bound indeed to question seriously the universities' ability to train the leaders we need, and we do well to

[1] See Julien Benda, *La Trahison des clercs*, Grasset, Paris.

ask whether the spirit of *la trahison des clercs* has not actually invaded their lecture halls and laboratories. We cannot conceive the quest for a New University without asking not only what ideal of learning it should advance, but also what kind of an *élite* it should endeavour to form. And this goes deep. It cannot be determined merely by reference to the social concepts of an epoch, nor yet by the dominant characteristics of a national genius. It depends ultimately on what we believe to be the true nature of man. The university, having clarified its idea of truth and of learning, must define its ideal of man.

The third constituent in the character of a university we found in the economic, social, and political structure of its land and epoch. As we survey the leading universities of the West, we become aware that this, which should be a secondary factor, has to a disastrous extent become primary, and subordinated to itself the ideas both of knowledge and of man. In some countries, as we shall see, it has done so completely, in others the chaos of society has generated a corresponding chaos in these primary ideas, and even in the countries least affected we see the consequences of this reversal of values. A parallel may be found in the frequently deplored condition of the Church during the War, when Christendom witnessed national churches identifying themselves with their countries' policies, and unable to hold above the mêlée a single idea of Truth and a common loyalty to God.

Rebels and Reformers

Fortunately the creations of life are never altogether true to type—and our universities are not yet dead. There have always been rebels, even in the time of the scholastics and during the domination of the encyclopaedists, men who have refused to conform, who have stood between the present and the future. To-day there are probably more of them than ever raising a voice in protest against the false types of university which are being foisted upon the world. In some countries, like Italy and Russia, they have grown so powerful that they have already completely transformed their universities. Nevertheless the situation is one of very real danger, and nothing reveals it better than many of the well-meaning proposals for 'reform' which have been made in recent years, especially in Germany and America. All too often they are confined to the purely external, technical aspects of university education. Some would lengthen the period of study, others shorten it; some would stiffen examinations, others abolish them altogether; some want economics taught in the faculty of philosophy, others in the faculty of law. All these things have their importance in their proper setting: apart from it they are more likely than not to miss the mark. But such a setting is impossible as long as a general conception of the university is lacking.

Proposals which aim at a re-creation of the university on the basis of such a general conception are few and far between. Men to-day lack the religious fervour which inspired those who in the midst of political and social disintegration created the University of Berlin, or those who ushered in the reform of the French universities after the defeat of 1871. Their thoughts turn back more often than forward to find the golden age of the university. To some it is the age of scholasticism, to others of humanism, to others again of romanticism, or of positivism; for each of these marked a period in which the idea upon which the university was built answered the uncertainty of man.

Needless to say these proposals originate mostly with people who consciously took part in the life of the pre-War world. The situation becomes tragic when we turn to the younger generation. They have no tradition to help them. The War has broken the link which tied the old world to the new. They find themselves thrown into a chaotic world without a past and, as it appears to many of them, without a future. They are met by teachers whom they do not understand and who do not understand them; for they belong to different ages, different worlds. The War has done its work thoroughly—there are hardly any bridges over the gulf. The young are hungering for leadership, and there is hardly a man to lead them; they long for certainty, and there is no idea that can grip them. Some try to escape from the torture of uncertainty by considering their studies only as a preparation for gaining a livelihood. They amass an enormous knowledge of facts; they pass one examination after another, despite the fact that for most of them there will be no employment. Others drift aimlessly from course to course in the hope of finding some answer to their inner restlessness, and find none. Is it any wonder that, while remaining formally citizens of the *civitas academica*, their minds turn to prophets in the streets whose apocalyptic visions or entrancing descriptions of the promised land lift them out of their physical and mental misery? They feel that these prophets are nearer to reality than their teachers, and that out there in the streets there is something new in the making, which will shatter all the syllogisms and formulas of the schools.

This tendency to centre their interest upon matters and activities outside the universities is strongest in those countries where the break with pre-War times is most complete, such as Germany and some of the other Central and Eastern European countries. Here not only has the continuity of educational ideas been broken, but most of the social and political facts which affect the university have changed. It is very different in France with her self-sufficient intellectual culture. The War has not succeeded in breaking the continuity of the humanist tradition, and plans of reform are on the whole confined to an adjustment of the university

to the needs of a developed democracy. Problems of access
to the university and of selection are in the foreground.
England also is less deeply affected. The students in Oxford
and Cambridge have been saved from the uncertainty of
their Central-European fellow-students by that liberal
education which postulates the development of character as
much as the training of the mind, and which expresses so
admirably the genius of the British nation. It would have
needed more than the War to break this genius, and to
shatter the community of living and learning found in the
old British universities. The modern English universities,
however, suffer from lack of purpose and maladjustment to
social and political conditions in much the same way as the
German universities. In the United States the situation is
somewhat different. Here there has always been a strong
tendency to make the universities into service institutions
for the convenience of a comfortable democracy. An *ad hoc*
pragmatism, translating itself into a tendency to make
learning subservient to immediate practical ends, and the
desire to give a minimum education to a maximum body of
students have reduced the universities to the level of advanced
schools. They have undoubtedly fulfilled a function in
building up American democracy, and the importance of
this cannot be overrated. But the cause of pure learning has
suffered. There are, however, encouraging signs. Not only
have American universities, despite their handicaps, produced a number of eminent scholars whose intellectual
achievements compare favourably with the best achievements
of contemporary European universities, but there is also at
the present time a growing intellectual restlessness amongst
professors and students, a dissatisfaction with the existing
colleges and universities and their methods. Apart from
Germany, there is no country to compare with America for
the number of books and articles appearing on the purpose

of the university. By professors and by students the most
fundamental issues of higher education have been raised.
It is time that European intellectual circles ceased to look
down upon American universities and colleges, and sought
instead their co-operation in the common quest for a New
University.

The Broken Unity

The quest for a New University—is there any ground for
anticipating that the institutions of higher learning, in spite
of all their national differences, will ever again be fundamentally united by one idea of knowledge and a common
ideal of man? We are not prepared to answer this question
in the affirmative. The essays of which this book is composed
would rather indicate that the last vestiges of unity are
rapidly disappearing. They appear to be studies in national
psychology rather than essays on the common essence of
the universities. Thanks to the services rendered by the
translators, the articles, some of which were originally
written in French, German, Italian, or Russian, offer an
extraordinary insight into the different national modes of
thinking. The Italian's eloquence, the German's love for
abstract thought, the Frenchman's clarity and precision, the
Englishman's sense of the actual, all are there. It seems hardly
believable that when the authors consented to collaborate
in the symposium they all undertook to answer the same
questions, to follow the same outline.

As their mode of thought differs greatly, so their very
conceptions seem to be altogether disparate. It is a long way
from Professor Fantini's conception of liberty in the Fascist
universities to the liberty of learning which, according to
Professor Bouglé, is an outstanding attribute of the French
university. Equally, concepts of the university which derive
respectively from Mussolini and Karl Marx can hardly be

said to tally. Altogether, the book seems to bear out our former contention that of the constituent elements of every university—its ideals of learning and leadership on the one hand and the economic, social, and political conditions of the community on the other—the latter have outdistanced the former in importance.

At the same time we witness as a phenomenon of first-class importance the revival of man's desire for the absolute. Professor von Hildebrand's passionate denunciation of 'science without presuppositions', and his attack upon the various disintegrating forms of learning based upon this idea, will meet with the grateful understanding of many who do not share his Roman Catholic convictions. It explains the recent growth of Roman Catholic influence in the world of higher learning, whether in the form of the establishment of Roman Catholic professorships, or the foundation and development of Roman Catholic institutions of higher learning, such as Nymwegen in Holland or Salzburg in Austria.

This same desire for an absolute, though springing from altogether different roots, can be seen in Italy and Russia. In both we notice a complete break with the 'liberal' tradition of the self-satisfied bourgeois whose conventional morality only barely covered his lack of principles in the philosophic sense, and in whose mind all values were therefore relative. The break with this tradition has not come about, as in the case of the Catholic idea of the university, through the acceptance of a timeless idea of knowledge, derived from the existence of a supernatural entity, an idea which exists irrespective of and even in opposition to the social and political systems of the day. On the contrary it is based upon the fact that these social and political systems have themselves been declared 'absolute', and that learning in order to be true must therefore fit into these systems. Just as the

Italian university sees in the Italian nation of to-day and in Mussolini its creator and symbol an embodiment of National-ism, which it conceives as the one true philosophy of life, to which all learning must be related, so the Russian univer-sity with equal conviction sees in the ideas of Marx and their embodiment in Soviet Russia supreme and absolute truth. It is as part and parcel of these 'absolutes' that the university claims, for its idea of knowledge, absolute and universal validity. Seen from this angle, it becomes perfectly compre-hensible that Russia views its 'old-time' intellectuals with suspicion and that Italy asks of its professors an oath of allegiance to the Fascist régime. Not to conform implies not only high treason to the State, but is tantamount to betrayal of the idea of learning itself.

A brief analysis of the Italian situation will show the implications of this position, which has given Italy a new religion, with Mussolini as its God and the Italian national state as his kingdom, a twentieth-century revival of the religion of ancient Rome. In the first place Fascism has inspired ever new efforts in research, for every new scientific achievement carries with it the supreme reward of being taken as a new proof of the greatness of the Italian nation. Not only the individual scientist, but the whole nation rejoices in it. It has furthermore infused a spirit of enthusiasm into the universities; a sense of fulfilment characterizes the new *élite* which is being created. It has removed doubts and uncertainty without quenching the thirst for new knowledge, it is increasingly giving the students and professors alike a sense of 'liberty' which induces them to make ever new sacrifices for the Duce and the nation. As Professor Fantini's article proves, there is no contradiction for them between the very strict control the régime exercises over the universities and that sense of liberty. On the con-trary, there is liberty because there is an absolute authority, which has established a new ideal of man. To that ideal they are wedded, and the marriage ring is not felt to be a fetter. To live in a state of liberty does not mean to *do* anything one likes to do—that is the old liberal idea—but to *be* something. To be something, however, presupposes the knowledge of what to be, in other words the existence of an ideal of man. The more this ideal has the sanction of the absolute, the more will man be able to reach that state of liberty in which he can live the ideal without any doubt or uncertainty. Thus, the Fascist Italian would reason, Mussolini, by positing the ideal of the 'New Italian', and by entrusting the Italian universities above all with his creation, has given to the universities that supreme liberty which they had been lacking before. However strongly one may feel concerning this 'false' religion, one cannot but admire many of its results and the thoroughness with which it has been applied.

Schematically, the Russian position is so similar to the situation in Italy that it would only lead to tedious repetition if we were to analyse it separately. The parallel between the 'New Italian' and the 'proletarian man' is evident, however far apart these two ideals may be. Russia, however, is even more consistent than Italy; its new religion is more intransigent than that of Fascism. In Russia the universities are centres of the 'Godless Movement', whereas Mussolini has reached a compromise with the Vatican which safeguards a certain amount of Church influence over the universities in purely spiritual matters: a lame compromise which satisfies neither side.

In countries like Germany, England, and France the situation is not nearly so clear. There are no theological principles universally accepted, no socio-political systems established, that carry with them the claim of the absolute, and which can protect the universities against the invasion of the *clercs qui ont trahi.* On the other hand, the whole tenor of Professor Bouglé's article implies the continued existence of the humanist ideal of learning in France; Professor Barker states that 'philosophy and universality remain the Alpha and Omega of British Universities', and Dr. Doerne says for Germany that 'the determination to achieve a humanistic *universitas* is not yet dead even in the youngest generation'. In other words, the universities have not abdicated, they still maintain that they have an idea of learning and an ideal of man which justifies their existence and distinguishes them from mere training-schools. The distinguishing criterion is to be their 'humanism'.

It is not, however, the humanism of old, which believed its learning to have absolute validity, and which carried with it an ideal of man because it found God in man, and the world in God. It is something much more modest, something which lacks the sanction of the absolute. To many it means not much more than a common knowledge of the Greek and Latin classics, a taste for clarity and precision, the lucidity of a mind trained in the ancient philosophies. This, however, obviously does not exhaust the meaning of modern humanism as applied to university teaching. In its most ambitious form it attempts to synthesize the various ideas of learning of which the human mind has conceived in the past. It is positivist in so far as it believes in science without presuppositions, it tends to obliterate the difference in method between the natural sciences and the humanities, it accepts on the whole reason as its arbiter, and it even tolerates the *intellectus speculativus* as long as it does not start from a dogmatic basis but from known facts. Fundamentally, however, it is empirical. It claims to look at things as they are, unhampered by a philosophical or theological *parti pris* about what they *must* be, and refusing to indulge in the antics of *a priori* 'reasonings' unverified by facts. It is essentially sceptical, for the absolute either does not exist or it is out of human reach. This very common attitude—which is a philosophical consciousness and not a new uniform philosophy—has its very strong sides. Its adepts can discard at any time former findings and theories and proceed to new hypotheses, to new testing, to new findings. It leads to continuous progress in knowledge of men and the world in so far as they can be dissected and measured and put together again, classified and pressed into statistical data, and in so far as one thing can be explained by another.

The great weakness of the attitude lies in the inadequacy of its conception of man, the stressing of his intellect to the exclusion of other sides of his nature. Education, under humanistic influences, tends to develop only the intellect of the student. This does not mean that it has no formative influence upon character, for no one can deny the interaction of intellect and character, but it does not grip the whole man. It does not tie him in loyalty to anything but a method, which may lead to ever new hypotheses but which cannot replace in full a scale of values based on the belief in something absolute. In times of stress like the present this weakness becomes particularly apparent. A great deal of tne strain and stress of German university youth, for instance, is due to the fact that the humanistic university is offering them in the whole field of human relations nothing but hypotheses. To their anxious doubts concerning the destiny of mankind, of Western civilization, of the German people, the historian has no certain reply. Similarly the sociologist, the economist, the ethical philosopher meet their questions with answers which are shattered by the next day's realities. No wonder that the universities are not bringing forth the *élite* for which the German nation is clamouring, and that strong tendencies towards a purely utilitarian opportunism prevail.

This weakness is not quite so apparent in France and in

England; in both these countries the universities are still producing an *élite* (in England this applies particularly to the older universities). There are in the two countries two different sets of reasons for this phenomenon.

It must not be forgotten that when the French speak of their *élite* they mean the intellectual leaders of the country— i.e. they stress those qualities, that very side of man which the modern humanistic attitude to learning is indeed cultivating and developing. The whole system of competitions which surrounds the institutions of higher education in France emphasizes, to the practical exclusion of all other considerations, the intellectual abilities of the candidate. It is during that period of the year 'when half of France is engaged in putting the other half through examinations', that the French *élite* is being selected. It must be remembered further that in France, more than anywhere else, humanism has not been confined to the universities, but has become an integral part of French civilization, and has penetrated the thought and action of the whole nation. Its roots go deeper than in other countries, and many of them reach down to that first period of humanism which carried with it not only a mode of thinking, but a way of living. It implies the acceptance of certain principles such as *la bonté*, *la justice*, or *la gloire*, which, though they may not have the sanction of the 'absolute' and are very much open to interpretation, serve as guide-posts to human behaviour. The dangers of the humanist tradition in the French universities are modified by these facts— though they have not altogether prevented the young *élite* from being contaminated by utilitarian, narrowly practical, or party considerations, as is proved by the fact that the cry of the *trahison des clercs* went up in France first of all.

The *élite* of the British universities—if one may give such an un-English name to something so thoroughly British—is being formed not so much by a definite idea of learning as by a conception of life. Its virtues can be best expressed in terms of life—personality, character, will-power, statesmanship, resourcefulness, courtesy—and, at least in the older universities and increasingly also in the modern universities, the best method of education is found in 'living together'. This makes it exceedingly difficult to analyse the world of thought of the British universities. In their methods of research, in their idea of learning, they are undoubtedly strongly influenced by the kind of humanist conceptions which have been described. At the same time certain elements which in themselves are extraneous to the humanist conception have been so integrated into the life of the universities that it is practically impossible to separate the two strains of thought. Consider, e.g., the role played by religion. A comparatively short time ago the University of Oxford was open only to students belonging to the Church of England; equally significant is the fact that the Student Christian Movement in Great Britain is spiritually more influential than any similar movement abroad. The curious combination of insularity and empire-consciousness, which constitutes the national pride of the British, is another formative element. Fair play and other conceptions of good behaviour are upheld with a conviction approaching religious fervour. All these elements together constitute what we have already termed the genius of the British nation, which finds a remarkable expression in the universities. Whether this unity of life and thought will withstand the disintegrating forces of the modern world remains to be seen. That there are certain dangers ahead Professor Barker has clearly stated.

It would serve no useful purpose in this introduction to go fully into the situation in America. As will be seen from the two American contributions to this book, the United States possess so many different types of university, the ideas of their purpose are so conflicting and at the same time so changing that it would be practically impossible to draw any general conclusions. Besides, such generalizations could hardly yield anything new, for the constituent elements of the American universities are to a large extent, though in varying proportions, the same as those of the European institutions of higher learning.

The Future

In order to evaluate our results we shall adopt the attitude of the saner element among the post-War generation in the universities. They are neither optimistic nor inspired by an undue pessimism; they are realistic and try to see things as they are. We have admitted that the unified conception of the university, which characterized earlier periods, has been broken. It is to-day no more than a memory and a hope. Whether, or in what form, this hope will materialize, it would be folly to prophesy. It does not depend upon the universities alone. They have no monopoly of the mind and there are other forces moulding our destinies. All we can do, therefore, in conclusion is to trace certain possible lines of development.

In the first place, and theoretically speaking, the universities of the world might accept, as do the Catholic universities, an already well-defined *Weltanschauung* with a timeless idea of knowledge derived from the existence of a supernatural entity, which would define not only the presuppositions of learning but also the ideal of man. There is no doubt that such an idea, independent as it is of historical change, would offer the strongest basis for a new unity.

Another possibility is that the universities should abandon all idea of putting forward an ideal of man, and confine themselves altogether to the cultivation of the intellect and the knowledge it can acquire. In other words, the universities might unite on a minimum programme which would imply little more than the common application of certain methods which we characterized when we spoke of modern humanism, leaving the formation of the *élite*, apart from intellectual training, to outside agencies such as the churches or divers idealistic forces. Keeping in mind the reservations made, this is a situation which applies already to countries like France, Great Britain, Germany, and the United States. It lays the universities open to invasion by the spirit of *la trahison des clercs*, a danger from which even the more deeply rooted conceptions of humanism cannot altogether save it.

As a third possible line of development we have witnessed the acceptance of new absolutist conceptions of the universities, which are not based upon timeless ideas of the beyond, but upon certain social and political systems, certain sociological notions which are regarded as absolute. This obviously tends to accentuate the differences between the various university systems, to separate them altogether from each other, certainly as far as their ideal of man is concerned, with which the idea of learning is closely bound up. If this is indeed the way our universities are going it must inevitably lead to conflict. No two 'absolutes' can for very long exist side by side. Again, theoretically speaking, one of these 'absolutist' systems may gain a victory over all the other systems. It is, for instance, conceivable, though not likely, that the communist or the fascist *Weltanschauung* may prevail owing to circumstances external to the universities, e.g. a successful world revolution. Such speculations, however, hardly serve any useful purpose.

What is essential here and now is that we should keep the channels of intercommunication open between the various systems. While there may be at present no unity of thought there must be a free flow of ideas from university to university, from country to country. Such an interchange of ideas will help to deepen and to clarify the existing conceptions of the universities, it will stimulate ever new efforts in the search for truth, with or without the sanction of the absolute and reached by methods which accept or refute presuppositions; it will safeguard them from the *trahison des clercs*. But it may do even more. Is it indeed impossible that the time may come when the elements of truth which are ours already will combine again in one overwhelming system of thought, transcending all boundaries of space and all socially or politically conditioned forms of the 'absolute', uniting again what hitherto has appeared disparate and chaotic? Is youth in all countries altogether wrong when it yearns after a new conception of the world, a *Weltanschauung* which will give it a firm point of departure for the establishment of a new order, wherein man and matter alike may be brought under due control?

The French Conception of the University

By C. BOUGLÉ

(Associate Director of the École Normale Supérieure in Paris.)

UNIVERSITY is in French an ambiguous word—and the
ambiguity is significant.

In the singular the word designates all those whom the
State has authorized to teach. Whether they be in university
chairs, in secondary schools, or in the primary schools of
village or town, all certificated teachers despite differences
of diploma and inequalities of salary belong to a single body,
a single department of State. In this unity there is doubtless,
as in so much of the French administrative system, a survival
of the will of Napoleon: the Emperor would have liked
to keep his teachers in hand like a regiment, making them
march together as one man. No one to-day dreams of such
a militarization of the university in France. But there has
developed out of the system another characteristic trait, viz.
secularization. Since with us Church and State are separate,
all members of the university are secular officials belonging
to a State department. That is to say that, while free to hold
their personal opinions, their public functions are liberated
from all control by the Church. One must at the beginning
recall this thread of destiny running through our history.
For centuries, long before the French Revolution, the
Catholic Church had fought with the temporal power over

the prostrate body of France. The remembrance of so long
a battle could not, with the best will in the world, be effaced
by the stroke of a pen. That is why so often when Frenchmen
speak of the university as a unity, as a corporation, they seem
to set it over against the Church, as though one of these
powers must be a perpetual menace to the other.

The universities in the plural signify the gathering together
of several faculties in a single place for the imparting of
higher education and the development of culture. Those
who reorganized our universities were far from letting themselves be hypnotized by the necessity of defending the State
against the Church in order that the State might be the
defender of intellectual liberty. They had other things to
think of. Yet they could not rid themselves entirely of
that which our history imposes upon us, and secular sentiment reveals itself as intimately bound up with national
sentiment in the soul of the founders.

There is no doubt that national sentiment, over-excited by
the defeat of 1870, became after that date the dominant
motive: wounded patriotism was one of the authors of our
university renaissance. Men were fond of repeating that we
had been beaten by the German school-teacher, and that
the universities had forged for the German states armour
both shining and strong. Renan in that painful examination
of conscience entitled *La Réforme intellectuelle et morale*
never tired of pointing out for our admiration the blessings
of that high culture, with its centres so happily scattered
through the land. Liard and Lavisse heard the warning,
nor were they to forget the models held up to them.

But before organization could begin, it had to be decided
in what matters liberty should be allowed in higher education.
And immediately the eternal problem reappeared: would not
the power of the Church force back the power of the State?
Louis Liard observes, in his book on *Higher Education in*

France, that except for a few Liberals whose imagination
saw all manner of institutions blossoming from the new law,
no one in 1875 could blink the fact that freedom in higher
education would profit almost none but the Church. The
way out was in compromise. Liberty was proclaimed for
higher education: any group whatever could open a college.
But the State would retain the granting of degrees: for
instance, only juries composed of professors from State
institutions might grant teaching certificates. On this point
Jules Ferry, the minister who, aided by Paul Bert, was to
organize the French elementary school on a secular basis,
compulsory and free of charge, opposed vigorously both the
bishops and their defenders. He maintains that though he has
no desire to set up a 'dogmatizing State, a State which should
be a doctor of philosophy, mathematics and literature', yet
since none can refuse to the Republic, 'guardian of the
national unity', a certain right to supervise the trend of
higher education, the right of granting degrees is the least
it should be allowed to retain.

The opponents of the project did not fail to observe that
to limit in this way the freedom of higher education was to
give with one hand and take away with the other. Other
than State institutions, since they would not enjoy the right
of awarding the diplomas that admit to the liberal professions,
would see their students melt away. Inevitably they would
become—free, indeed, but handicapped, not to say paralysed.

As a matter of fact the Churches have been able to maintain or even develop under the new régime certain institutions of higher education which are penetrated by their own
spirit. The Catholic Institute of Paris recently celebrated
its jubilee with great brilliance, and demonstrated the services rendered both to science and to faith by its students
and by its teachers, of whom some like Branly are famous.
The Protestant theological faculties have seen their prestige

increased by the 'return to the fold' of the Faculty of
Strasburg.

Nor is it only the Churches who have benefited by the
liberty granted. In the Students' Handbook of the University
of Paris one notes over thirty independent institutions of
higher learning. Among them l'École Libre des Sciences
Politiques deserves separate mention. It was founded in
1871 by Émile Boutmy, encouraged by men like Hippolyte
Taine, who wished to see a more positive spirit dominating
youths who were destined to set a nation on its feet, a spirit
more realistic than that of the official university, which to his
mind was too literary. The School endeavoured to provide
recruits for the higher grades of the French administration.
It attracted at the same time, both from home and abroad,
many students who merely attended its lectures. Abroad it
has won an established reputation—so much so that the
Germans were wont to say that the diplomats it had formed
had largely helped France to win the War. Let us rejoice
that the German Hochschule für Politik, which was founded
on the analogy of ours, is endeavouring, through the International Institute of Intellectual Co-operation, to come to an
agreement with the École Libre on the subject of equivalent
degrees and such exchange and collaboration as may serve
the cause of peace.

But however interesting may be these efforts to take
advantage of the freedom of higher education, it remains
true that in France the 'official' institutions are of prime
importance. They are the best equipped and the most
frequented: by the mere fact of the diplomas they confer,
they set the tone and standard for the rest. So that it is the
State institutions which France has multiplied and co-
ordinated that one must visit if one would measure what she
has done for the promotion and spread of culture.

. . . .

The man who won the victory for the university in our country was Louis Liard, seconded by Ernest Lavisse, whom he himself has called 'the Fichte of our regenerated universities'. To understand what has been attempted in France since 1870 in the way of intellectual renewal, one must go to their works: Lavisse's *Questions d'enseignement national* or *A propos de nos Écoles*; Liard's *Universités et facultés* or *L'Enseignement supérieur en France*. The necessary instruments of this renewal were the universities, whose faculties had to be grouped together in order to co-ordinate their teaching and research. The faculties until then had been isolated and were becoming sterile in their isolation. In order to achieve this reform Liard was not content to evoke the glory of her universities which France had enjoyed during the Middle Ages; he tried to demonstrate that the Revolution, too, had desired for them a similar glory, that its thinkers had worked for the progress of human culture by the *rapprochement* and interpenetration of the sciences.

The universities of the Middle Ages had shed upon France an incomparable lustre. It was chiefly on account of the masters who gathered on St. Geneviève's Mount that Paris was called the City of Letters, the Queen of Sciences, the dwelling-place of the divine Muses. At the remembrance of so many student 'nations' meeting on the sacred hill to applaud Abélard, Eudes de Châteauroux could exclaim: 'Gaul is the oven in which the intellectual bread of the human race is baked.' In the fourteenth century men went so far as to say: 'The Pope and the University of Paris are the two lights of the world.'

But whether it were Paris, Montpellier, or Toulouse, the vitality of our universities was not maintained as the centuries went by. Their story under the old régime was one of progressive decadence.

It has been shown that on the eve of the Revolution science

was developing without them, if not in opposition to them.
Sap was lacking in the old tree, which yet had thrust such
deep roots into our soil. And so it was that the men of the
revolutionary assemblies did not hesitate to cut it down, or
rather to let it fall. They intended indeed to replace these
anaemic corporations by bigger Schools, both more accessible
and better equipped. Talleyrand projected a huge teaching
Institute, to promote letters and arts, as well as science. Con-
dorcet, preoccupied not only with bringing the elements of
education within reach of all, but with perfecting the human
spirit, planned nine *lycées*, where future professors and
scholars should be trained. The spirit of the *Encyclopaedia*
presided over these conceptions. One finds in them the same
sense of the oneness of Mind, of the solidarity of the sciences,
of the services of every kind that those sciences can render
to the nation. These are the traditions to which the renova-
tors of French university life love to appeal. They present
the reform which is so dear to them not as a return to some
form of the old régime, but as a logical manifestation of the
Republican hope.

'Our modern universities will differ from those of the
Middle Ages', wrote Ernest Lavisse, 'in the absolutely contrasting principles that inspire them: the Middle Ages
subsumed all spheres of knowledge under theology; our age
ranges them under science. The Middle Ages lived by
authority; we by liberty.' But who forbids us to remould
the old bottles in order to pour new wine into them? The
re-created universities, not only in Paris, but in Montpellier,
Toulouse, Bordeaux, Lyon, Lille, will aid the human spirit,
as it searches after truth in many directions, to become
conscious once more of its unity; and at the same time they
will give back to the intellectual life of the provinces the
animation and interest which all too often have completely
fled.

For the object of the reformers was indeed a double one; they aimed at once at centralizing research and at revitalizing our provinces. Long before, when a faculty of medicine was created at Reims, Victor Cousin had formulated these two aims as clearly as could be desired:

'It is the intention of the Government to create in France a certain number of major centres of higher education, to become focuses of light for the provinces in which they are placed. Isolated faculties may have their advantages, but they can develop their maximum power only by uniting. A Law Faculty can hardly function without a Faculty of Letters, and a Faculty of Science is at once the basis and the completion of a Faculty of Medicine. Thus it is that all human knowledge is bound together, and its parts support one another and impart to those who cultivate them an education both sound and broad, the true illumination of knowledge. Nor is it a matter of indifference, socially and politically, that we should retain in our provinces numbers of young people whose talents, matured in the great schools of their land, may be turned to her profit and help to form or strengthen that provincial life which used to be so animated, but is to-day so languishing, and whose return would be a blessing, without in any way being a danger, to the powerful unity of France.'

This intention was carried out: seventeen universities were created in France in 1896. To what extent did they satisfy the double hope in which they were founded?

First of all, was the effort to relieve the congestion of Paris a success? Were any steps taken to bring about this intellectual decentralization? Many Frenchmen loudly regret the impoverishment of our local life. The mighty edifice of unity, raised not only by the Revolution or the Empire, but—as Tocqueville long ago demonstrated—by our kings first of all, crushes with the whole of its weight this fragile plant. Do the provincial universities provide for it a means of escape? They have all they need, or so it would seem, to function freely. They have their own budget, administered, under the presidency of a Rector, by a University Council which includes elected members as well as a certain number who sit on it 'de jure'. The deans of faculties are elected by their colleagues. The universities can receive bequests, control funds, create chairs, found laboratories and institutes, and respond in a variety of ways to the needs of the regions which are mirrored in these their universities.

Two years ago, at the seventh centenary of the University of Toulouse, over five hundred professors drawn from all over France, and from all parts of the world, had the opportunity of admiring several adaptations of this kind. Not that they are likely to have found many live traces of the university whose foundation they were celebrating. Too much water for that has flowed under the bridges of the Garonne since Cujas, Raymond de Sebonde, and Sanchez. Above all it must be remembered that the rose-red city had witnessed, even under the old régime, the slow and irremediable decadence of her University. Nevertheless, the university was united by century-old bonds to the City, and in asking the latter to make sacrifices for her sake, the university could evoke a past of glories shared.

It is a remarkable fact, too, that at the time of the Revolution, when it was a question whether the University of Toulouse should not be suppressed, a native of Toulouse outlined a regionalist programme which to-day is more up to date than ever. In his memorandum, preserved in the archives of the Upper Garonne, this clever lawyer of the year VI indicates all that a system of higher education could aim at in Toulouse, if it would both bring to light the hidden vestiges of a glorious past, and at the same time answer to present local needs, look around it and give its attention to the mountain, the rivers, the plain, and set free their slumbering wealth.

This is exactly the programme of the University of

Toulouse to-day, justly proud as she is of her new co-ordinated faculties and of the institutes she scatters over the province. The Observatory, the Electro-technical Institute, the Institutes of Applied Chemistry, Agriculture, and Child Welfare, all these live enterprises give an impression of intellectual activity which is indeed applied to life and which adds to the will to discover the will to serve.

The institutes thus controlled by the university are eighteen in number. The Faculty of Arts alone had in the year 1925–6 nearly six hundred students. These figures prove that in university matters at least decentralization is not quite an empty word.

In similar ways more than one provincial university has profited by the possibilities of renewal which the law of 1896 opened up. Witness, e.g., the Brewery School and the Chemical Institute at Nancy, the Electro-technical Institute at Grenoble, the School of Watchmaking at Besançon, or again the courses on France and her culture that are organized for foreign students by Grenoble or Dijon. Monsieur Hauser, a fervent regionalist, could in 1924 conclude that the law of 1896 concerning the universities had powerfully aided the regionalist movement; it had not only decentralized, but actually regionalized intellectual effort.

But let us not hasten to proclaim the victory won—over Napoleon, over the Revolution, over Louis XVI, over all the powers, detested of Proudhon, who laboured to centralize France! The framework of the building they erected still holds. And whatever we may say, on this framework the universities continue to lean. There is the Rector, who represents in the University Council the Central Power, which is patron and donor, which imposes regulations at the same time as it gives grants. Compared with the State chairs, the independent university chairs are in an infinitesimal minority. The professors are always appointed with the approval of Paris. And it is a Consultative Committee meeting in Paris—surrounding itself indeed with all possible guarantees—which decides who may teach in the universities, and who shall receive promotion. Most of the competitive examinations for the whole of France, which give access to a goodly number of careers, and for which the universities prepare their students, are held in Paris: among others the *agrégation*, which must be passed by those who wish to become secondary school teachers. In Paris again is held the competitive examination for entrance to the École Normale Supérieure and the university scholarship examination, which reserves the head of the list for the University of Paris, and sends only a few scholarship winners to provincial universities. Finally, it is in Paris, in the Louis Liard Hall, that the best theses for the State doctorates are almost always defended. Nearly all the candidates wish to go to Paris to be examined and show what they are capable of. How different from the British or German systems!

We recall how, when we were at the École Normale, an English friend, who had asked three or four of us to accompany him on a visit to Paris, noticed from our conversation that we all counted on returning and finding each other there at some future time. And this appeared to him an evil and a great danger.

The danger, if it is one, is nowhere near being circumvented. True, with the help of raised salaries in the provincial universities, we see to-day more and more professors deciding to stay in their own provinces. But, generally speaking, Paris wins, Paris the Unique City, who, as Louis Liard used to say, attracts and engulfs us all.

.   .   .   .

As they stand, whether in Paris or in the provinces, can we say that the universities have attained the second objective set them by Lavisse and Liard: have they promoted higher culture and worked for the advancement and expansion of the sciences through the fructification of science by science?

When several faculties unite to form a university, a variety of tasks becomes incumbent upon them, which it is not always easy to reconcile. In one sense they remain professional schools: they open the way to certain liberal careers by training lawyers, doctors, professors. At the same time their professors—especially those of the faculty of arts—are required to keep in touch with non-university audiences who like to keep abreast of these men's studies; such is the function of the public lectures. Again, it is desired that every professor of university standing should be a researcher, should set an example, should contribute his quota to the subject he teaches, be it chemistry, archaeology, or what not. This means that our universities must be lecture-halls, seminars, and research institutes all at once; or, if you will, that our professors are invited to become Jacks-of-all-trades.

Complacently the picture has been drawn again and again of the intensive life led by our universities to-day, as contrasted with the slowness of the days before university reform. Those which give public courses of lectures continue to attract the faithful, often in large numbers; and this maintains between Town and Gown an intellectual interchange and currents of sympathy which are not to be despised. More important, our teachers now have teams of young research students whose work they direct while they initiate them into their own subjects of study. A great novelty this and a great gain. Unfortunately it must be added that the best part of the teachers' time is passed in preparing these young people for examinations, competitive and otherwise, and that the programmes of these examinations determine the activities of the teachers as much as of the taught. There is one period of the year, it is said, when half of France is engaged in putting the other half through examinations!

There is something in the jest. Examinations do occupy
the front of the stage with us, and they weigh heavily upon
all our work. It is a burden which is very hard to shift;
probably because the average Frenchman, being an equali-
tarian on principle, has a holy horror of anything arbitrary.
If a position is not allotted by competition, if, e.g., the master
is allowed to judge and classify those whose capacities he
has been able to test personally in his laboratory or his
seminars, immediately we raise the cry of nepotism. One
man will suspect local, another central influence, one the
influence of the *curé*, another that of the deputy. Examinations and competitions exist as guarantees to that thirst for
justice which devours the masses of our people. For this
reason candidates and examiners cannot hope yet awhile to
be delivered from the plague so often denounced.

A last charge against these practical preoccupations is that
they sometimes interfere with, if they do not sidetrack, the
energy for scientific work in our universities. In our arts
faculties, when at one and the same time students have to
be prepared for degrees, for diplomas, and for the *agrégation*,
even the broadest shoulders find themselves heavily bur-
dened. Were it not for vacations—happily fairly long—
when the professor can refresh himself at the pure springs
of learning and replenish at leisure his stock of ideas, the
years would pass without his completing any of the personal
research which is demanded of him; vacations are indeed
his shield and buckler against the deadening routine of
teaching. Realize again, however, that if he is insufficiently
paid our professor must seek outside work, and it is clear that
in this case you will have all too soon a man who is wholly
used up and lost for the cause of science.

Let us hasten to add that such cases are still rare. University professors for the most part pride themselves on doing
personal research. From this point of view one cannot praise

too highly the practice of writing theses—those theses of
which the University of Paris shows with pride so huge a
collection. These literary monuments are oftentimes admirable and at the same time terrifying; terrifying for their
sheer mass, for the days and nights of labour embodied
in them, for the expenditure they represent; admirable for
the extent and depth of the researches undertaken, for the
methods employed, for the talent devoted to them. Most of
those who have survived this hard test are anxious to widen
the path they have opened up. They retain a taste for private
research and a desire to attract their scholars to it. In this
sense it is untrue to say that the concern for examinations
and competition in the reformed universities eliminates
completely the concern for research. Provided that the staff
is sufficiently large and varied, a French university can still
carry off with success the manifold tasks laid upon it.

We cannot estimate the cultural possibilities afforded by
the French university, unless we take into account, in addition to the universities properly so called, those schools and
institutes of ancient or modern foundation which are in a
position to collaborate with them.

The Revolution killed the universities, or more exactly
allowed them to die. It tried to put in their place Schools
with general or specialized programmes; Central Schools,
one in every Department, and in Paris Special Schools like
the Muséum or the École Normale. It has often been
repeated that the university system and the system of big,
specialized schools are mutually antagonistic. It would have
been more logical to choose between them. But in this
matter of education the French have so many different
historical traditions to respect at once, that it is very hard
for them to be logical. For instance, the historian, Ernest
Lavisse, conducted a campaign against the Polytechnic, a
small faculty of science, where they admittedly overdo

mathematics, and the mathematician Paul Appell followed suit. But their attacks soon wore themselves out. The Polytechnic as it stands, hybrid though it is, training for both military and civilian careers, has rendered too great services and provides our leading circles with too many good servants for it to be possible seriously to think of changing it from top to bottom. It can claim, too, that it gives to the *élite* whom it stamps with its spirit a general culture of a mathematical type which is no negligible force, once application has corrected its abstractions.

The École Normale Supérieure has appeared to be more affected by the reform. In order to avoid overlapping it was attached in 1906 to the University of Paris; it was deprived of its permanent lecturers; its students, now regarded as holders of scholarships lodging in the Rue d'Ulm, were simply to follow the courses of the Sorbonne. But the École Normale survived the shock. It is likely indeed that its scope will henceforth grow rather than diminish. At a time when a large number of universities all over the world are trying to establish or restore the collegiate and tutorial system, i.e. to have picked students living together and working in teams under the guidance of teachers by whom their work is closely followed, it comes home to one that these two advantages are already combined in the Rue d'Ulm. On the other hand its stiff, competitive entrance examination, which includes three written dissertations (literary, philosophical, and historical), two translations (one from Latin and one from Greek or a modern language), and one Latin composition, has the merit of encouraging youths in those preparatory classes, intermediate between the *lycée* and the university proper, which characterize the French university, to achieve not only variety of knowledge, but above all elasticity of mind. They have every opportunity to acquire, in addition to the art of presenting ideas clearly and in order, that general knowledge of the humanities which is the best preparation for advanced studies.

If again our young men outside the walls of the Sorbonne, *Normaliens* or others, wish to take up specialized, advanced studies, there are the courses of the Collège de France, founded by Francis I for the love of learning. The Republic has multiplied its professorial chairs with intent to permit scholars to carry on their researches and produce new work in all liberty, with no examinations to preoccupy them— their only obligation to keep the public informed of their discoveries in lectures whose number is expressly limited. And then there is the École Pratique des Hautes Études, founded by Victor Duruy, as a reaction it appears against the eloquence of the public lectures revelled in by the arts faculties of his time. Here there is but one desire, to know the truth, naked and unadorned. There is direct collaboration with the students, the professors using their help in concrete work for the advancement of science. The School aims above all at copying the form and preserving the character of a workshop.

We must close this enumeration; it is long enough to give an idea of the variety of means at the disposal of the Third Republic for the propagation and the promotion of learning in its higher branches.

.   .   .   .

But what of the result, it will be asked, what of the influence of all these courses, lectures, and experiments on the minds of our educated youth, on their aptitudes and tendencies? This one would like to know; and just this it is extremely hard to say with any exactitude.

Every time I have read an inquiry on the youth of France, whether before or after the War, I have observed with surprise that hardly any of the general conclusions of the inquirers are borne out by my personal experience of the

young people I have known. Such discrepancies warn one
to be circumspect.

For this reason I should be at a loss to reply to the
questions which many of our contemporaries are anxiously
asking. Is general culture on the down grade? Is humanism
lost? Some conclude that because the faculties of arts have
split up their degrees into separate certificates they are
good for nothing more than the manufacture of specialists,
possessed of much knowledge but limited in outlook and
with no comprehensive grasp of things. Others insist that
the evil is due to the reforms of 1902, which by prematurely
specializing the boys in the *lycées*, and above all by opening
the universities to those who had neither Latin nor Greek,
dealt a fatal blow to French culture.

I must say that in the circle known to me I cannot believe
French culture to be in such bad case. I perceive indeed that
the best of our future arts students have some trouble in
producing as correct Greek translations or Latin composi-
tions as their seniors did. It cannot be denied that it would
mean a stiff pull to reach the former standard in these
subjects. But in French, in philosophy, in history—at least
among the students who have passed through the preparatory
course for the École Normale Supérieure and the degree
scholarships—no general weakening can be observed. These
young people certainly know more than their seniors, nor
does it appear that they present what they know any less
skilfully. The taste for clarity and precision is still dominant
in a large number of them: the characteristics of French
thought remain on the whole intact.

Can this be proved? We should perhaps ask the question
rather of our foreign observers, especially those who, like
Señor Salvador de Madariaga, have had the privilege of seeing
representatives of the various European cultures meeting
face to face. In Geneva debates, is it not always said that the

Frenchman stands out as clear in expression, logical in argument, clothing his remarks in beauty of form? In those meetings, commissions, conferences I see plenty of Frenchmen who were not twenty years old in 1902. Their minds were moulded by that reformed system which is so much abominated by certain people. Can any affirm that they have emerged from it markedly ill trained?

. . . .

Nevertheless it is fear of the mortal danger run by that humanism which is the very strength and grace of French culture that incites some of the best minds to resist all efforts at enlarging the role of 'democracy' in our universities, all efforts at opening university studies to the largest possible number of gifted children from the lower classes. And thus arise some grave problems, whose solution we do not yet see: e.g. the so-called 'primary invasion', and the State school question.

It is said that for the children of the people access to the higher realms of culture would be facilitated, if those who went through the elementary schools could ultimately proceed to the university. A child begins in the elementary school, goes on to the higher elementary, then to the teachers' normal school—all providing free education. He has not been able to get into the *lycées* and *collèges*, where up to the present fees are required. If one day he finds that his tastes and natural gifts urge him towards the university, not merely to attend lectures but to take his degree as a regular student, he lacks that certificate which is the Open Sesame to higher education and the seal of a secondary education, viz. matriculation (*baccalauréat*). Matriculation is the proof of good work done in the *lycées* and *collèges*. Should the 'primary' achieve one of the alternative forms of matriculation which includes neither Latin nor Greek, or should he pass an equivalent examination (e.g. the first part of the teachers' examination for the primary normal schools) he still risks being stopped at the next rung of the ladder: e.g. if he wins in the faculty of Arts a 'free degree', consisting of three certificates and the teacher's diploma for primary normal schools, he will never obtain the *licentia docendi*, the right to teach in *lycées* and *collèges*, which presupposes, in all its many branches, at least a minimum of Latin.

Despite these obstacles a goodly number of 'primaries' do find a way of getting out at the top into secondary and higher education. The St. Cloud École Normale Supérieure d'Enseignement Primaire (Upper Normal College) has recently celebrated its jubilee. In the bulletin of its Friendly Society are to be found the names of two hundred and ninety of its scholars who have won diplomas and degrees of secondary and higher education. Fifteen are professors in universities or in the Muséum, a score are teachers in the *lycées* of Paris. There has, I believe, been no complaint of the way they fulfil their functions.

Nevertheless there are circles in which they and their like are viewed with suspicion, and to which it would be a matter of satisfaction to remove at least the title of *licencié* (Bachelor of Arts) from those who have won what is now called the *licence primaire*. These 'upper primaries' are looked upon as the advance guard of the 'primary invasion', the mighty wave which if you listen to some people is prepared to overwhelm our classical culture. These people still speak of 'the primary mentality' as of an indelible stain. The opposition thus maintained between classical humanism and 'primary mentality' is one of the characteristics of our university situation. Between the departments of secondary and of higher education collaboration is particularly easy in France, and one can pass freely from one to the other. Their staffs receive the same training in the universities and the École Normale. Many of the teachers in the secondary schools are preparing theses for the State doctorate, a degree necessary for teaching in universities and colleges. On the other hand, most of those who become university professors sit the competitive examination of *agrégation*, which gives the right to teach in secondary schools. The staffs work together on examination boards, e.g. that of matriculation, and in no country are their contacts easier, exchange of ideas more frequent, or collaboration more cordial. This is for us a notable privilege.

But between secondary and primary the demarcation is up to the present strongly marked. They are two separate worlds, which have neither the same methods nor the same mode of thinking. It is remarkable, e.g., that the primary student takes pedagogy seriously. The secondary student is apt to laugh at it. The elementary and higher elementary schools believe it worth while to devote a few hours to moral education. The *lycée* schoolmaster usually regards it as entirely unnecessary. The League for Moral Education, the president of which was Gustave Belot, inspector-general of secondary education, demanded in vain that moral lessons should be reintroduced in *lycées* and *collèges*, for do not these enjoy a humanistic culture? Many of our colleagues are not far from believing that that culture is the answer to every question. Whoever possesses it has every chance of achieving nobility of character and a distinguished mind. But he who lacks this talisman must always lack that synthetic view, that sense of general truths, and above all that critical spirit which is, especially in France, the salt of the earth.

Note that those who complain that the 'primary mentality' is narrow have not looked with a very favourable eye upon the efforts that have been made to enlarge and enrich it in the soil where it grows, viz. in the normal schools where the teachers of the future are pursuing their studies. Paul

Lapie, when he was director of primary education, took to heart the task of raising the intellectual level of these schools. He indicated the right methods for a renewal of their teaching methods and introduced not only the elements of psychology, but also 'sociological ideas applied to morality and education'. This produced a fine uproar, and Paul Lapie almost lost his job. He appeared to think that this renewed and enlarged education would develop among primary teachers that critical spirit and sense of relative values which, as his opponents assert, they so lamentably lack. The retort was made that he would succeed only in developing among them overweening ambition and incorrigible pride.

Was not the true remedy ready to hand? Why not send them to the *lycées* and *collèges*, these future primary teachers, instead of leaving them shut up in what M. de Monzie has called their 'secular cells'? In this way the unification of all the future educators would be brought about from above. And true culture would undoubtedly benefit thereby.

One suspects that this counter-offensive has not failed to awaken much uneasiness. The 'primaries' insist that their schools, whatever may be said of them, have their windows open on life, that while their scholars are glad to take advantage of university courses and lectures, their community life in close touch with an elementary school which provides direct contact with children, contributes not only to their intellectual but to their moral and pedagogical formation; this it would be difficult to achieve in the secondary schools.

However, the hare has been started and he will run a long while. Inquiries and counter-inquiries have begun. Reform of degrees and reform of the normal schools, these two related questions will cause much ink to flow and awaken strong passions on either side.

.   .   .   .

But the maximum of passion no doubt will be saved up

for the State school system, a capital problem, which is now in the focus of public attention, and will furnish a platform for the parties of the left in the coming electoral campaigns.

In our old scholastic edifice, has a stair wide enough been provided from one story to the next? Can a gifted child, if his parents have no means, pass easily from the elementary to the secondary school, and from the secondary school to the university? And is it not a scandal that the deciding factor should be less the capacity of the child than the wealth of his parents?

After the War this question, old as democracy, recovered its full urgency. The *Compagnons de l'Université Nouvelle*, mobilized teachers who had begun to think about it at the Front, pointed out that the memory of the 'brotherhood of the trenches' demanded at the very least equality for the children in the educational system; also that at a time when the nation was bled white and needed to exploit rationally all her resources, it was in the national interest and not only a matter of social justice, to train the best minds, wherever they might be born, for posts of leadership. On their side, the *Ligue française de l'enseignement*, recalling the wishes of Jean Macé, Jules Ferry, and Paul Bert, undertook an inquiry led by Ferdinand Buisson, into the methods of organizing the State school system. A committee was elected to work out the practical possibilities. Édouard Herriot set to work. In his plan the elementary classes in the *lycées* were to have the same programme and the same staff as the corresponding classes in the public elementary schools. The secondary schools which resemble higher elementary schools would, like those, admit their scholars free. Free education would be extended gradually throughout all *lycées* and *collèges*, beginning with the sixth form. The day when the budget for this reform was carried was, as M. Herriot declared, a great and historic one: children gifted enough to proceed to higher studies would not henceforth see their advance cut off by the old barrier of money.

Doubtless M. Herriot and his partisans do not hide from themselves the great difficulties they still have to meet before the State school system is realized in France. The scruples of the humanists, the uneasiness of the Church and of a part of the *bourgeoisie* are so many spokes in the wheels of progress. Are you, ask the former, out of a mistaken love for democracy, going to tread underfoot Greek and Latin, to which incidentally democracy owes so much? You recognize that it is they after all which furnish to French culture its peculiar form and power. But in order that this culture may produce all it is capable of, there must be, in a famous phrase of M. Lachelier, a 'slow impregnation of minds'. We therefore need to begin nursing our future humanists very early in the secondary schools. Now in order to allow the children from the elementary schools to achieve this same culture, you force us to begin Latin later than before; you dream of a 'short Latin course' which will be insipid and valueless. And simultaneously you invite us to seat on the same benches, to learn French, children who have done Latin and children who know no solitary word of it. It is the old attempt at 'amalgamation'. No proceeding could make our efforts more sterile, for it robs us of the incomparable aid which knowledge of the Latin texts provides for the understanding of the French texts. Under cover of smoothing the course for the majority, are you not holding back your best minds? Do you want to rhyme democracy with 'mediocracy' and have it imply the predominance of quantity over quality? The argument seems to appeal to many humanists, even when they are democrats. And in the last report but one on the education budget we see M. Ducos, who is an excellent democrat, supporting his colleagues in secondary education in their repugnance to 'amalgamation' in all its forms.

But other and more serious difficulties suggest themselves. We find here again that struggle for influence between Church and State, whose gravity in France we have mentioned; we hear once more their debates concerning the freedom to teach. Does not the talk of State schools appear to favour the complete restoration of the teaching monopoly, the closing of all private educational institutions? And we have shown with what energy the Catholic Church, the great provider of private educational institutions in France, clings to the right to teach, since it can no longer hold in its own hands the teaching monopoly. Touch that right and you will be accused of letting loose a civil war.

The opponents of the State school do not miss the opportunity of exploiting this ambiguous situation. If you wish to bring about equality of opportunity in education, say they, you cannot in the nature of things confine your measures to State institutions alone. Yet if you extend them to Church institutions, they will be tyrannical. This was a dilemma on the horns of which M. Léon Bérard, the late Minister of Education, used to rejoice to impale his adversaries. 'The State school system', he was wont to repeat, 'is impossible without a monopoly, which is impossible!'

The Radicals endeavour to avoid this conclusion. They protest that the two problems remain absolutely distinct. And for their part—whether it is that the freedom to teach seems to them logically linked up with freedom of thought, which is dear to them above all else, or whether they feel it inopportune to relegate all power and initiative to the State —they declare themselves ready to allow to private instruction, whatever its tendencies, every latitude to carry on its experiments. M. Ferdinand Buisson agrees on this point with M. Édouard Herriot. And M. Poincaré was able to reassure public opinion in the Chamber of Deputies: until further orders the monopoly of education in France is but a phantom to scare men, a phantom evoked on purpose for the fight against the State school.

Suppose this ambiguity dissipated; we shall meet another obstacle on the road. This is a sentiment which fears the light of day, but is not the less active for that: unavowed sentiments are not the least powerful. We speak of the alarm felt by a good proportion of the right-thinking and well-bred *bourgeoisie* at the prospect of having its children mix with those of the people. The State school apparently means in the first place mixing of social classes, children of all origins elbowing each other on the same benches. And there are people who are terrified of mixing and elbowing. There are 'contacts' one legitimately desires to avoid. This was the revealing statement made by M. Augagneur in the Chamber. We need hardly say that few Ministers at the present time would dare openly to support their arguments with such considerations as these: we live no longer in the age of M. Thiers.

But there is another prospect to face, a further matter for alarm. Can free education produce those happy selective effects which are expected of it? At the passage of arms witnessed by the Chamber last year over the education budget—the discussion of this budget always occasions a tournament of oratory—M. Jean Mistler, a young radical-socialist, made a speech of which we shall long hear the echoes.

He insisted on the necessity and at the same time the difficulty of selection in a State school system; and he tried to prove that without selection free education would be ineffective. It would not bring about in secondary education that renewal which many desire to see. A deplorable over-crowding would sterilize the whole innovation. By trying without careful planning to introduce into the schools the policy of the open door, we should be herding a mob into a cul-de-sac.

Methodically M. Jean Mistler produces statistics to support his argument.

In the sixth form of the *lycée*, where education has this year been made free, 22,000 new scholars have entered instead of 16,000, an increase of 37 per cent. In higher education, instead of 42,000 students we have to-day 73,452. If the increase continues we may foresee for 1940 a number three times as great as we had before the War.

Try to imagine what these two figures signify, one taken at the base, the other at the apex of the pyramid of higher education. For the young men who complete their studies we must anticipate many a disappointment, for it is doubtful if positions can be found for so many graduates. This means so many more *déclassés*, so many more rebels on our streets. Meanwhile, for the children who continue their education in the *lycées*, which form by form will soon be offering a free education, overcrowding will be the rule. The classes will contain not twenty-five or thirty pupils, as they should, but fifty or sixty or more. There will not be enough class-rooms. And even if new schools could be built in time, well-equipped masters would be lacking. The French university would run the risk of a lowered standard as well as an overflow of students.

Is it wise then to open wide the sluices? Free education without selection means accepting every Tom, Dick, and Harry; it means the mass of 'duds' blocking the way of the gifted and preventing us from offering to the latter a culture worthy of them. It is constantly said that democracy, more than any other form of society, needs an *élite*; can it truly be said that this is the best way to form that *élite*?

If overcrowding occurs at the top, viz. in the universities and the careers they open up, shall we not necessarily be forced to introduce the *numerus clausus* which M. Jean Mistler has observed functioning in Central Europe, where it is said to lead to so much injustice? Should we not be tempted to leave the door to higher education no more than ajar?

The conclusion would seem to be that it would be far wiser to weed out the unfit on the threshold of secondary education. Do not admit those who have no hope, those who it is clear will derive no real profit from it. Take all the precautions you wish in measuring your candidates' chances of progress in a prolonged course of study. If you are suspicious of examinations, let these candidates be observed carefully during their last year in the elementary school. But in one form or another a test must be imposed; free education without selection means a hotch-potch in our schools.

But by thus systematically tying together these two terms, *free education* and *selection*—as firmly it would seem as Herriot used to tie together *disarmament* and *security*—it may be guessed what uneasiness, what wrath the distinguished university deputy will arouse. Free education may pass. Nearly every one to-day admits, nay welcomes it in principle. In the report, full of substance and flavour, which M. Ducos devotes to the education budget, he takes a wicked pleasure in enumerating the adherents gained by this principle which he has defended for so many years. Does not M. Léon Bérard himself admit that the present school system 'subserves one of the most cruel of social inequalities', and that the idea of opening the highest culture to talent, wherever it may originate, 'cannot fail of a response from every just mind and generous heart'? M. de Waren echoes his words: 'Every French child must reach, according to his aptitude and regardless of his parents' position, the full measure of intellectual and moral achievement.' M. La Cour Grand-maison, M. François Saint-Maur, M. de La Cases, Canon Desgranges in their turn say Amen. We are in good company.

But show the other side of the shield. Specify that the State school system demands selection of the scholars who shall enter. Then the tone changes. Halt! Out upon the learned asses who claim to measure in childhood the capacities of our sons! The rights of the family, repeats M. Louis Marin vehemently, would be cruelly outraged thereby. In vain we shall try to quote in this connexion a formula of M. Léon Bérard: 'Intelligence must be sought where it is to be found.' This same M. Léon Bérard warns us that the State school system with selection is 'a variant of the assault upon the *bourgeoisie*, the expropriation of one class by another'.

M. Ducos observes innocently that the dreaded sorting process takes place already. For instance, in this or that higher elementary or vocational school it often happens that the number of candidates for admission is greater than the number of places: many of the candidates are therefore rejected until further notice. Why should it be a scandal to institute a similar selective process in secondary education? Why this indifference concerning primary or technical education, why such indignation when secondary education is in question?

The reason is perhaps simple enough. The families whose rights M. Louis Marin defends with the energy we know, are for the most part families who can pay. And that which seems so scandalous is that a father who can pay should not be allowed to keep his son at the *lycée*, however much of a 'dud' he may be, until a too easy matriculation examination opens to him the way to the university.

Here is the stumbling-block in the way of the State school, and all the reformers of to-day come up against it. Whoever can remove this stumbling-block will have accomplished a labour of Hercules; and may boast of having brought about a veritable 'revolution'.

E 2

Problems of the German University[1]

By MARTIN DOERNE

(Director of Studies in Lückendorf, Saxony.)

The Foundations of the German University

THE German university in its characteristic form is a creation of the university reform of 1809, but originally it had its roots in the common strata of western tradition. Towards the end of the Middle Ages, on the models of Paris and Bologna, the Universities of Prague (1348), Vienna (1365), Heidelberg (1386), and Erfurt (1392) were founded. Their organization is not distinguishable from that of universities in other civilized European countries. Ecclesiastical philosophy, canon law, together with a desultory inheritance of antiquity in the scheme of the *septem artes liberales*—all this, bound together with monastic forms in a community of work and social intercourse, makes up the medieval university.

From these common sources of Catholic internationalism the manifold special forms of the national university in modern times have developed. The so-called *Landesuniversität* or provincial university leads the way for Germany from

[1] This article was the result of detailed discussions with Professor Theodor Litt at Leipzig, who declares himself in agreement with all the main points of the essay. In consideration of the close co-operation which produced this contribution, individual quotations from the books and essays of Professor Litt were not included.

the *Studium generale* of the Middle Ages to the modern university through a particularly German stage. It is called to life in the sixteenth and seventeenth centuries principally upon Protestant territory with definite political and confessional aims. Of this type of university are Wittenberg (1502), Frankfort-on-the-Oder (1506), Marburg (1527), Königsberg (1544), Helmstedt (1576)—for the greater part, as one can see, situated on east and north German territory. All these universities are State institutions, in a stricter sense than originally were their medieval predecessors. Their history follows with many changes the course from the confessional State of the sixteenth century, with its elements of guild and feudal government, to enlightened despotism. The State guarantees the connexion of academic teaching with the creed of the country in so far as it is interested in the matter. The heritage of antique scholastic philosophy remains, however, for the university as general educational material, in the form in which it was recast and handed over by Melanchthon.

The deeper the modern spirit, the spirit of the Enlightenment, of independent learning, pierces into the system of Protestant life, the more severely is the type of old provincial university shaken. Halle and Göttingen become the apostles of the new rational and critical spirit, which is on the point of dissolving the traditional connexions. On the other hand, however, the very existence of the universities is questioned by the popular scientific, philanthropic, and utilitarian currents of thought towards the end of the eighteenth century. Their task of research has already been taken over in the seventeenth century by the academies. In so far as they are places of professional and technical education, their functions are to be taken over by special training schools, which must be founded on a new basis.

At this critical juncture in their history, simultaneously

with the dissolution of numberless old universities in the Napoleonic period, a movement begins, which not only saves their outward existence, but for the first time gives the universities in general their classical German character. Its basic force is the new theory of *German Idealism*, essentially evolved by the *New Humanism* deriving from Winckelmann and classical poetry. This theory, together with the humanist ideal of education implanted in it by Humboldt and Schleiermacher, provides the university once more with a foundation, which it had lost since the Middle Ages. A *universitas literarum*[1] again arises which finds its unity in the material unity of learning itself, and moulds its internal organization into a pure learned community, as the social form which corresponds to this unity of knowledge. 'Only where the essential unity of all learned research was proclaimed, could the form of the university also find its highest justification' (E. Spranger).

It was Fichte and Schelling who created this great new conception of the university and developed it systematically. Their metaphysics of the intellect (*Geist*) place the scholar personally and actively in the universal process of history, and make him the priest of the Divine Reason which rules equally in nature and history. The university is henceforth founded in idea on three principles:

(1) All knowledge is essentially one,

(2) All reference to an extraneous aim is opposed to the very essence of learning,

(3) Scholarly work is service to God and at the same time to the whole of civilization.

The university has accordingly philosophy as the 'principal constituent of its life-structure'

---

[1] *Universitas* or *universitas literarum* is used in German to describe the universe of knowledge and its embodiment in a university.

This ideal, transcending time and nationality, in which the united German and Hellenic spirit offers its gift to humanity, is, however, realized and individualized under special historical and national conditions.

The final impetus comes from the internal rebirth of the Prussian State, of which the Stein-Hardenberg reforms are the political expression. The men at the head of this movement, amongst them in the first place Fichte and Schleiermacher, see the prospect of national freedom closely connected with the task of intellectual and moral reform of national life. Here finds expression a national idea which desires through an idealistic system of education to raise and purify the German spirit until it becomes a pure embodiment of humanity. In the university plans of Humboldt and Schleiermacher, political liberalism, the German transmutation of the ideas of the French Revolution, at once gains an influence over the university. Its internal life is made independent of the State. At the same time the administrative and financial connexion with the State is preserved, without a restriction of its internal freedom being apparent. Until to-day in Germany we have no private universities.

As the purest representative of this new type the University of Berlin is founded in 1809; in 1811 Breslau follows, in 1818 Bonn. The new type henceforth influences the further development of the older universities. The German university now receives as its most distinguished characteristic a *strict reciprocal connexion between research, teaching, and learning*. Research and teaching are necessarily related, because the realm of knowledge by its very nature is not a sum of readily transmissible results and formulae, but is ever growing and becoming, and is only realizable at any one time through free individual activity. The metaphysical dignity of learning at the same time makes scholarly work the highest form of education into true humanity. \The dower of the university to its scholars, the education to pure knowledge, brings at the same time a moral purification and ennobling of the student. This education is also of peculiar value for vocational training, and thus gives to the 'academic' professions a mission to humanity, which extends beyond all immediate aims of the profession or of the State, and is held in almost religious veneration. Thus the Idealistic idea of the university binds together harmoniously the individual will of the nation and the State with the will to achieve universality. It has its roots in 'Germanity'; but the national consciousness which it inculcates among students is in no way at variance with the idea of humanity. The connexion of the university with the State is not regarded merely as a chance relic of older times, but there is a clear consciousness of its incorporation as a State university in the whole of national State life; at the same time it holds fast jealously to that academic freedom which it has received from the Idealistic conception of liberty, and would consider the sacrifice of this possession in favour of chance needs of State or society as a violation of a sacred trust.

In any endeavour to reach a deeper understanding of German life one must return again and again to this idea of the university; it remains the most characteristic form of the German national spirit. Its dignity, but also its danger, lies in the elevation of its ideal. It is clear that there is need for high intellectual and moral exertion on the part of the nation —and above all of the students actually in the universities—in order to keep alive and develop the heritage of this ideal for successive generations. Not always, not in all branches of academic life has this exertion kept pace with the demands made upon it by the idea: the discrepancy is often only too painfully visible. Nevertheless, during more than a century of her history Germany has realized that she is committed to and responsible for this conception of the university.

Transmutations in the Idea of the University

The German university is born of the spirit of Idealistic philosophy. But it is not thereby eternally obliged to adhere to a definite dogma. This spirit is sufficiently adaptable to be able to absorb the most diverse developments of learning. Above all it has a positive relation with the manifoldness and irrationality of the *historical* world. Thus it continues its influence in the great jurisprudential, historical, and philological achievements of the so-called historical school as an inspiring force, long after the breaking up of its classical systems. True, it is ever more manifest in the course of history that the unifying bond of the university is not to be sought in changeless philosophic principles. But, amidst the continual increase and differentiation of the spheres and methods of the specialized sciences, the idealistic heritage asserts itself as a common theoretical attitude, as a striving after purity and comprehensiveness of knowledge.

A break in the development, a threat to the *universitas* first comes with the rise of *positivism*. Let us attempt to describe this change shortly.

At first it may seem as if the positivist theory of knowledge were eminently suited to be a foundation for the *universitas literarum*. It rests on the principle of pure rationalism, as worked out and tested in the classical development of natural science in the seventeenth and eighteenth centuries, and applies the process of rational abstraction, which has here established its efficacy, indiscriminately to all forms of reality. An imposing unity of method! The promising beginning of a synthetic comprehension of the whole realm of experience.

But this new *universitas* of untrammelled research operating without presuppositions, is dearly bought. Metaphysics, in the perfection of which Idealism thought to reach for the first time the unity of the world of experience, is excluded from the work of science, the vital mutual connexion between Man who knows and the world which is known is torn asunder. Instead of a *universitas* of the mind we have a well-ordered catalogue of facts and laws, laws which are not those of the living human being. As explanatory psychology and sociology are set up as the common basis of all mental and historical science, the freedom and the irrational individuality of historical life are denied. Thus the connexion between learning and *Weltanschauung* as well as that between learning and education loses its innermost necessity. The realm of actuality and the realm of values are dissociated. Education can no more, as formerly, be universal education into the full stature of humanity. And at the same time, despite all desire for synthesis, the paths of the individual branches of learning are forced farther and farther apart. The desire for realism alone remains as a connecting link, and even the idea of truth, which is still written on the banner of research, is transformed and restricted until it becomes the mere gathering of facts.

And does the desire for pure knowledge, at least in this reduced form, really remain the driving force of 'positive' science? Is positivism the consummation of a realism which works without presuppositions? Or do the gaps left in its inner structure leave an opening from the very beginning for the influx of utilitarian and practical tendencies outside the realm of learning? Is the watchword *savoir pour prévoir*, *prévoir pour pouvoir* the prelude to a compulsory development of positivism into *pragmatism*? The questions which arise here are of decisive importance for the future of the German idea of the university.

An answer can only be found in conjunction with an analysis of the *new life forces* which since the third and fourth decades of the nineteenth century begin radically to reshape the European world. It is apparent that positivism is only the theoretical exponent of these life forces, and that the changes in the university idea, and the menaces to it, have not their most profound cause in a revolution of learning, but in a revolution of the whole of civilization. The world has never been a world of poets and thinkers, as little in Germany as elsewhere. But it has been reserved for this new era, which is now dawning, with a consistency quite remarkable to see in 'Civilization' (that is, in the rational domination of the world) the very meaning of culture, and thereby to force the humane world of the spirit on to the very periphery of cultural life. The impressive upgrowth of modern technique creates new horizons of existence, purely of this world, and absorbs men's creative forces chiefly in the sphere of practical life. The national State organizes and centralizes itself more and more rigidly into an imperialistic State. The rapid increase of the population compels the State to spend more and more of its energy in aiding the people in their struggle for economic expansion. While Europe as a whole speeds towards sharper and sharper conflicts and thereby accelerates and disturbs the rhythm of national life till it is close on bursting-point, a similar disturbance is caused from within by the complexity of social conditions, the increasing heat of social and economic debate, the formation of a revolutionary working-class and the concentration against it of the great capitalist forces. The 'neutral' sphere of life, so necessary if academic culture is to thrive, grows ever narrower, and it seems ever more hopeless to try and keep the world of the mind out of this struggle of present-day forces and interests, and upon it to build up a living conception of solidarity for Europe and for the nation.

The question, What will become of the Idealist conception of the university? expands at this point into the broader question, What significance and what value can learning have at all for the building up of the nation, of society, and of culture? To be sure, the age of rational domination of the world is unthinkable without the effective collaboration of learning, above all of natural science, which is an indispensable instrument of technical and industrial expansion. Science thus assumes unparalleled importance. Scientific institutions are promoted on a magnificent scale, new colleges are founded for technology and commerce, societies for physical, chemical, and biological research are formed, men fondly hope that the solution of all social problems will come from the development of science. But it is just this cult of science that reduces it to subserving the needs of a purely utilitarian 'life'. It is to assist us 'to acquire domination over matter by calculation' (M. Weber). And what is the consequence of this reducing of science to a mere means? It is only too clear. Science is no longer an adequate foundation for educating the whole man, especially for a generation of youth which is scattering into a multiplicity of new professions. The 'academic type' threatens to become a phantom, the ideal of the *universitas literarum* to degenerate from being a reality of experience to which one owed a profound obligation into being a mere subject for ceremonial speeches.

Passage through the realm of learning now signifies for untold numbers liberation from all unconditional authority. Where everything is causally 'explained' there is no room for an absolute which can demand our allegiance. The fundamentally analytical attitude which works out in the humanities as 'historicism' (i.e. the explanation of everything by history) produces that relativist view of life, that *anarchy of values*, which renders it completely problematic whether learning has any function of ethical education to perform. Parallel to this runs the process of *specialization*. The immense increase of scientific material produced by exact research, and still more the positivist renunciation of all attempt at incorporating the particular in the whole, makes the connexion of learning with life in the deeper sense ever more slight and meagre. And the realities of European political and social history meet these tendencies half-way. The more one accustoms oneself to see 'reality' as determined by economic, social, and even biological events, the more is one inclined to cast doubts on the independence of learning, and as the final triumph of 'enlightenment' to interpret all intellectual conceptions as mere reflections of a material world. The Marxian doctrine of the 'ideological superstructure' is a classical example of this process. Pragmatism, which is tantamount to the suicide of learning, seems to be the inevitable end of this development.

The process here touched upon, which is surely at the root of the present 'crisis of the university', has not yet come to an end. Specialization and the disintegration of knowledge proceed unceasingly, and their effects on the life of the German university are immensely accentuated by the material need of the times, to which we shall have to give special consideration in a moment. Nor does the mental state of the world in which we are living seem to be moving towards any radical reaction.

In so far, however, as the university crisis is a *crisis of learning*, promising signs of an internal revival are to be observed. German learning is pressing towards a new unity, a new realization of the autonomy of the mind. One might describe the development now in process as a combination of two at first sight opposing forces. On the one hand, especially in the natural sciences, we are experiencing an *intensification of relativism*, which, however, is not leading to absolute scepticism, but is forcing us back to a profounder and very fruitful consideration of the foundations of learning, both in method and content, and so charging them with a new philosophic significance. And alongside this inner transformation of science, which reinstates dethroned Philosophy within its own rights, another current flows, and mingles with it, a current which has its sources outside of learning and can be described as a *reaction of Life*, of Man against the intellectualization and mechanization of the modern world. Nietzsche was already amongst its heralds; in our own day it is represented by the youth movement and by the vitalistic philosophy. It is a protest against the splitting up of human existence into separate professional branches; in a new romantic atmosphere the longed-for image of past ages is conjured up, together with the vision of a 'new man' who is to come. A new education of the personality is demanded, in which all knowledge will but aid a man 'to come to himself' The dualism of 'is' and 'ought', of observation and evaluation, must disappear in a new synthesis which offers both knowledge and regulation of ethical conduct at one and the same time, offers in short a new *Weltanschauung*.

These demands for the most part go far beyond what it is possible for learning to give; this is clear from the nebulosity of the university ideals which issue from this quarter. Yet from the fusion of these currents with radical relativism a new phase in the history of learning emerges, which opens up also promising prospects for the idea of the *universitas*. This is most clearly seen in the progress in method which has been made in the humanities. The line of development starts with Nietzsche and proceeds through Dilthey, Windelband, Troeltsch, to Spranger, Litt, and Rothacker, and it has its parallels to a certain extent in phenomenological philosophy (Husserl, Scheler), in so-called existential philosophy (Griesbach, Heidegger), partly also in the new departure in evangelical theology (Barth, Gogarten). The conception of learning as operating without presuppositions is shaken to its foundations, the ideal of an exact objective knowledge of 'reality' is revealed as a mere illusion. The unescapable 'perspectivity' of all forms of intellectual conception of the world is realized. But with that very realization, in opposition to positivism, the mind which knows and the world which is known again enter into close relationship. By freeing the world of the mind from the bonds of the scientific dogma of causality, learning again becomes human and must steep itself anew in the consideration of its own philosophical basis. E. Spranger has a masterful description of these transformations in his treatise *Der Sinn der Voraussetzungslosigkeit in den Geistes-wissenschaften* ('The meaning of the absence of presup-positions in the humanities'). His results must prove painful to the positivist dogmatist of learning. But for a conception of learning and for a conception of the university which regards lively activity as a promising sign and recognizes in the radical examination of the principles of knowledge the humane function of learning, they will not signify disillusion-ment but hope. We must sacrifice the superstition that learning as such can give us a philosophy of life. 'But we do believe that to-day an intellectual and moral life can no longer be led unless it is illumined by the light of learning and purged in its flame' (E. Spranger).

The Present State of the German University

Yet it seems hard to-day to make favourable forecasts for the future of the German university. To the crisis of learning, the dangers of which cannot be over-estimated, the *crisis of the university as an educational institution* must be added. And we shall see that the German university is particularly severely affected by this crisis.

This crisis has its basic cause in the intellectual and spiri-tual transformation of the more recent student generations. The significance and the mission of academic study, as we have understood it from Humboldt on, can only be realized if we presume that the young men who come to the university are possessed not only of good general talent but of a scholarly cast of mind. A certain percentage of practically minded students can always be carried along in the stream. But if this practical and professional-minded type gains the upper hand among the students, the existence of the university appears to be seriously menaced. One cannot deny that this menace is to-day actual fact.

One is tempted to trace the changes in the student body to an analogous change in the *system of secondary education*, and not least to the change which has occurred in the university qualifying examination. After 1918 new types of secondary schools were introduced, not in strict accordance with a set plan, which have patently facilitated for the practical minded the access to a university. The late professor of English philology, W. Dibelius, also complained of an insufficient grounding in facts in many secondary schools. Thus it is that to-day the salvation of the university is often expected from a reform of the secondary schools: a more stringent method of selection, a unification of the examination system. Yet with all this one should not forget that the reasons for the change in the students lie very deep. In an age whose interests are almost entirely political and economic, it will not in the end be possible to prevent young men in great numbers from availing themselves of academic education to equip themselves for the struggle for existence; nor will these young men be taking the 'academic type' as their ideal in life.

This difficulty attains its full importance only when we realize that in the meanwhile the numbers of students in German universities have risen alarmingly. Thus it is that the problem of *overcrowding* stands in the foreground of all discussions upon the university. Some figures may help to show the gravity of this problem.

In 1914 Germany's universities had some 59,000 students, in 1930 they had 99,500; the technical colleges had formerly 12,800, to-day they have 23,700. The total, including the other professional colleges, amounted to 79,000 students in 1914, to 130,000 in 1930. The abnormal increase has taken place mainly since 1926; it amounts in this last half decade to some 45 per cent. The increase is almost exclusively in the universities, the number of whose students has grown during this period from 58,800 to 99,000. This process has been of alarming proportions in medicine, in philosophy and history, in mathematics and natural science, in jurisprudence and in dentistry. In some States elementary school teachers in training must be included, though in Prussia they are relegated to special training colleges. In the department of economics, which was filled to overflowing after the war, the tendency is retrogressive; in other subjects too a standstill has been reached. But even if it proves possible to prevent a further influx, the possibilities of employment for the generation studying at the moment in most branches will be quite hopeless. The number of unemployed graduates for 1934 is estimated at roughly 90,000. It would be instructive to call the attention of an international public to the grave dangers which this figure betokens for the social life of Germany. Here we shall make only a cursory inquiry into the causes of this inflation.

It is certain that there are some mitigating circumstances. H. Sikorski has set them forth in the enlightening studies which he has published in recent volumes of the periodical *Studentenwerk*. In the development of civilized peoples there is perpetually a certain relative increase in the quota of students. Further we must consider that the period of study in many subjects has been prolonged, either by new study regulations or indirectly by a higher standard of examination. But all these considerations do not deprive the rapid increase of its disquieting character. Should the new slogan of 'democratization of education' bear the chief blame? Certainly the revolution has had some democratic school reforms as a

result, e.g. a special examination for the talented, and the
'Aufbauschule'.[1] But they have brought the university only
a meagre percentage of increase. However, it is important to
observe that, in addition to the tremendous increase of women
students (18,200 as against 3,600 in 1914), the number of
students in the Prussian secondary schools has increased
250 per cent. during the last thirty years, while the number
of university entrance examination students has increased
even as much as three times. This is an expression of the
endeavour to rise in the social scale. It affects mainly the
middle class, while the proletariat up to the present plays but
an insignificant part in it. In estimating this state of things it
is common to criticize the hypertrophied 'qualifications system' (though the criticism by no means passes unchallenged),
that is to say the continuous stiffening of the requirements
and examinations for most posts in the State and in economic
spheres. Perhaps something can be done to improve the
situation. Yet the system of qualifications and the endeavour
to rise in the social scale perpetually act and react on each
other. We are dealing here with a process of differentiation
in cultural organization which appears to be an almost inevitable law of development for the European nations. There
is no doubt that the decrease in the relative birth-rate, which
also encourages the tendency to rise in the social scale,
couples itself with this law as a most disquieting phenomenon.

Stress must further be laid on the role of the *economic
crisis* in overcrowding the universities. Tens of thousands of
students are studying to-day simply because access to the
non-academic professions, above all to commerce, is denied
them. W. Dibelius is right:

'Formerly the rise in the number of students was a sign of increasing national well-being, to-day it is only a symptom of the

[1] A special form of secondary school intended to facilitate the access of
the poorer classes to secondary education.

most dire distress. The university is to-day a temporary haven of refuge for innumerable individuals who otherwise, as soon as their school years were over, would sink to the ranks of the proletariat. Since 1926, probably 30 per cent. of German students every year have entered the university for this reason. And one can imagine what a dangerous mass of inflammatory, revolutionary material and social embitterment are heaping themselves up now in those old homes of German culture.'

The reactions upon the internal form of the university are not long in coming. 'The idea of mass study is incompatible with the idea of the university' (Dibelius). The situation is paradoxical. The spirit of the time demands greater stress on the pedagogical side of university study, but at the same time, owing to the masses of students coming up, the possibility of personal contact between them and their teachers, at least in the principal subjects, is reduced to a minimum. The lectures have often to be transmitted by 'loud speakers' to several auditoriums. In the 'seminars' and institutes which are supposed to educate their members to a practical participation in scientific research, the vast body of students makes effective collaboration impossible for most of them. The *numerus clausus* and the appointment of supplementary assistant lecturers for the so-called 'Proseminare' or preparatory private classes are only a partial help. In many subjects, for instance in philology, a portion of the students needs further grounding; the line of demarcation between the top classes of the schools and the first year at the university is in many cases no longer clearly defined. Under these circumstances the standard of academic teaching is in danger. The professor is compelled in his lectures to adapt himself to the capacities of the students and the professional and practical direction of their interests, for the greater part of them to-day expect above all education for a profession. It is for this reason that the old system of study courses has had added to it new subjects which have grown out of practical needs. 'There are to-day numerous branches of study which are no longer strictly systematized, but require of the student only an empirical knowledge of a sum total of facts,' says Spranger. He mentions welfare work, adult education, modern languages, study of foreign countries, folk-lore, &c. It is possible indeed to fashion these new courses in the spirit of the university; in fact they offer a pre-eminent opportunity for realizing the aims of humanism. But it is hard for the university in addition to her regular functions to satisfy all these requirements, ever increasing with the progressive specialization of professional careers. It is all the harder when she is at the same time expected to develop the research work which is her own intimate speciality, and which also is undergoing progressive specialization. The teaching staff is so overburdened by the present state of affairs that the best qualified among them are almost excluded from the possibility of personal research. What then is to become of the university?

The anxious question must be repeated also in reference to the *students*. One can hardly reproach them to-day with not working industriously. The pressure of severe economic necessity weighs too heavily upon them, and very few are tempted to fritter away their time of study. The students passionately repudiate representations of student life which would give the impression that university days are still a time of care-free enjoyment. The attendance at lectures is more regular than ever. Time is scarce, and so is psychic energy, for 'diversions' which do not definitely belong to the prescribed course of study. For many students it is still essential to earn while studying. The transformation of the student type which has taken place in the last fifteen years is, however, not in every respect gratifying. For with the apparent freedom and unconcern about definite material ends, those imponderable treasures of academic freedom are also lost which used to determine the atmosphere and individual colouring of German university life. On this side too the university is threatened with the fate of dropping to the level of a school for professional education.

Plans and Efforts for Reform

So it is that many circumstances are working together to make the question of *university reform* particularly pressing for Germany. The tasks before us are of the most varied kind. The influx of the masses to the university must be limited. The selection of the talented must be more strict. The disadvantages of specialization must be compensated by new forms of instruction. Above all the university must make allowance for the change in the character and needs of the students as a body, without relinquishing its leading ideas. And all these efforts find their limits in the present over-crowding which it will certainly not be possible to overcome by administrative measures. We will attempt to make a short review of the plans and suggestions for university reform.

In *administration* and *internal organization* of the German universities the disturbed years since 1918 have brought but little change.

True, the question of the *relationship of the university to the State* was brought forward in a new guise by the revolution of 1918. Would the equilibrium of external association with the State and internal independence from the State, which had been characteristic of the German university since 1809, be preserved? This grave question has been answered in the affirmative by the developments of the past ten years. The 'liberal' ideas of the Reform of 1809 were restated in the constitution of the Reich in 1919. Only in those provinces in the governments of which socialistic thought gained practical influence, did tension between State and university from time to time arise. A not insignificant portion of German university teachers has constantly since 1918 seen academic freedom, the aristocratic principle of the university, endangered by the democratic and socialist ideas of the education authorities. There has, however, seldom been actual conflict. Nor could any definite change be expected from a realization of the so-called Reich reform, that is a centralized supervision of all German universities. In that case also the rights of the smaller universities (Rostock, Greifswald, Giessen, Erlangen) would presumably be preserved. It is only too clear to-day how overcrowding at the larger universities is endangering the very essence of study. The freedom to move from university to university, a peculiar advantage of the German university system, would be even further promoted by the Reich reform. A new situation would arise only if a government came into power which no longer respected the idea of free learning.

Even where the State has attempted to penetrate and reform the *inner structure* of the universities, tradition and the compulsion of existing conditions have been strong conservative influences. Prussia strove after the revolution to acquire for the assistant professors and the so-called 'Privatdozenten' or private lecturers increased influence in the academic administrative bodies (Faculty Councils and Senate). Yet the picture as a whole has altered very little. The sharp distinction between full and assistant professors has remained, likewise the high degree of independence of the faculties from one another. The 'Privatdozenten' have in some cases received salaried posts. But their unofficial position, which indeed bears with it the risk of a totally unassured existence, has been preserved in principle. It is regarded as valuable that the 'Privatdozent' should remain, in spite of the increased and varied staff of assistant lecturers.

After 1918 the *students* were largely incorporated in the body of the university. Shortly after the War representative bodies of students had been formed which were recognized both by the universities and by the State and were given the right to raise compulsory subscriptions. They united in a collective organization, the German National Union of Students (*Deutsche Studentenschaft*) corresponding to the 'Union of German Universities' (*Verband der deutschen Hochschulen*). At present indeed this organization includes only a portion of the students: also State recognition has been withdrawn from a considerable number of State branches of this organization (e.g. all those of Prussia) on grounds of political conflict. But where these branches still exist and are recognized, their representatives have a voice in the senate in all matters concerning the students and also take part in the election of the rector. The further development of the Union and of its organized connexion with the university is now hard to prophesy.

All the existing universities and other parallel institutions have been preserved; the universities of Cologne and Hamburg, and some specialized colleges have been newly added since 1919. From time to time it has been debated whether the technical colleges should not be reunited with the universities. Yet this idea, which was more especially espoused by Becker, formerly Prussian Minister of Education, has not been realized; there are good grounds in favour of separation. The technical colleges and the other specialized colleges which are run on similar lines (schools of commerce, veterinary surgery, farming, mining, and forestry) continue by their independent existence to remind us that the university conception of 1809 is no longer the only one in Germany. At the same time, however, the historical 'faculty' system has not been violated in principle. Only in the philosophical faculty has differentiation been carried farther, and even its two branches, the philosophic-historical and mathematical-scientific, have been subdivided. Some universities too have removed political science and economics from the faculty of law. There has certainly been no lack of plans for a radical and *systematic reorganization*. The separation of research from teaching is an important part of these plans. The late philosopher, M. Scheler, proposed in 1921 a total reconstruction along these lines: splitting up of the university into institutions for higher professional education, research institutes, institutions after the manner of the Collège de France (for synthetic treatment of the main branches of learning), and People's Colleges. But presumably all these plans will remain but plans. The intimate connexion of research and teaching remains the basis of the German university—a type which is complex, but in practice thoroughly justified. No one will ever succeed in organizing on a basis of pure reason and system this university which is 'with its contradictions, and through those very contradictions, a living spirit' (Th. Litt). It is a great mistake to suppose that the *universitas literarum* can be 'made' by systematized organization. Rather will the existence of the *universitas* always depend on whether the people who learn and teach there cultivate a vision of the Whole.

These considerations lead us on to the *internal problems* of university reform. Corresponding to the hard circumstances of the present day these present many and varied facets. Our exposition must draw attention first of all to the currents and tendencies which aim at a *spiritual renovation* of the Idealist *conception of the university*.

The *students* were keen participants in these tendencies, especially during the first years after the Great War. The generation that returned from the trenches to the lecture-rooms was filled with an all-embracing and fiery determination to reconstruct the whole of life. University reform was to them only a section of the universal reform they aimed at. They had felt the Great War and its result as a judgement upon the intellectual and remote-from-life attitude of the old academic world. They longed for lively contact with the whole People, they demanded a university which much more directly than before should equip its students for the service of people and State, which should educate 'characters', 'citizens', 'leaders'. The ultimate and most sincere desire of this generation, however, which calls in question all traditional bonds, is 'man'. Up till now there were professional men, drudges of power, slaves of business. Now upon the ruins of shattered civilization the new man is to rise, the 'full man' in harmony of spirit, soul, and body, bringing with him a new, genuine morality, helping to create the new, essentially 'human' society to which he belongs. From such impulses, which are very closely related to the ideas of the German humanism of 1800, and which gain a very practical expression in the *new humanism* which is central in Becker's writings on reform, there arose in student circles as early as 1919 the plan for a 'humanistic faculty'. This would take over in a carefully planned system of lectures the educational and political functions of the university, and thus give the student in addition to his professional studies the vision of Man as the embodiment of the *universitas* of the intellect. The restoration of the German university idea, the belief in a new man, the struggle against rationalism and specialism, social and national hopes —all intermingle in this plan for a humanistic faculty. The plan has had a changeful history. In the work of the so-called *Fachschaften*, student bodies representing the different branches of study, the humanistic current was united more and more with desires for a practical reform of professional studies. The severe tension between the humanistic and the practical and professional conception of Life was at first scarcely perceived by the university youth of the post-War years. Both forces worked closely together in the demand for *new forms of instruction*, which should help the student to do independent work, to come earlier into contact with his future professional work, and finally to have personal touch with his professors.

While the 'humanistic faculty' gradually disappeared from the reform programme of the students or was propagated only in reduced form as 'an organic co-ordination of public lectures', and while political controversies were more and more withdrawing the energies of students from questions of university reform, the discussion of this subject became concentrated increasingly on practical questions of a *reorganization of study and examination*. True that students have repeatedly projected overwhelming plans of reform; an analysis of the proposals made by the different political groups (Social Democrats, lately also Communists and National Socialists) is peculiarly illuminating here. But for the actual problems of the university these radical plans—the will being stronger than the power to achieve—serve no practical purpose. The German university will outlive such revolutionary storms, provided that it is within limits capable of evolution, and does not allow 'pure learning's Mount of the Holy Grail' (Becker) to degenerate against its own will into a domain for the old 'academic' type of individual.

The vital tasks before us lie in the *progressive development of forms of instruction*. This development, while ultimately anchored by the laws of learning and of its several branches, takes new directions in response to the changing educational needs of the students. Thus it is a matter of so far as possible adapting the forms of instruction to the needs of a changing student body, and preserving at the same time the inherited idea of the German university.

Mere academic conservativism is not enough. It is Utopian to focus the work of the university only on a small minority, for whom learning is their life's vocation. The selection is essentially a matter for the upper forms of the schools. The university for its own part, while furthering the study of its scholarly *élite*, must endeavour to help the main body of students to a serious understanding of the scientific and philosophic bases of their future callings. This obligation immediately excludes learned specialization from occupying the front of the stage in academic instruction, and it equally precludes the realization of exaggerated desires for a general humanistic education.

What are then the practical questions and requirements that will be principally served by such matter-of-fact reform of the system of study? The answer must naturally be very different for the various faculties and branches of study. The question of reform is to-day most acute for the humanities, which ideally constitute the core of the university. Here one must start from the fact that the intellectual and sociological basis for academic freedom in the present day has become very restricted. In the measure that the danger of anarchy in academic liberalism (Spranger) grows acute, the need arises for a strict *regulation of the course of study* in the humanities. And parallel to this run the attempts to *arrange the time of study* organically, roughly in three stages, of which the first would serve principally for the acquirement of facts, the second for approach to the essential problems of the particular branch of study and learning, the third for introduction to independent research. Every form of knowledge is of course an indissoluble whole, so that great difficulties stand in the way of the attempt to grade the course of study. It is also open to doubt whether the progressive differentiation of teaching methods—preparatory seminars, coaching, small study groups—whether this tendency to reduce the university to the school level is helpful to the development of a *civis academicus* who has reached intellectual independence. Nevertheless there seems to be a certain unanimity among arts lecturers and students that, while maintaining as far as possible the principle of the student's freedom to choose his course of study, a firmer regulation, a stricter arrangement of study is at the moment unavoidable. Spranger makes the following trenchant assertion: 'The organization of the studies of the humanities in the German universities is primitive. An American with his conception of the organization of university studies would smile at it.'

The reform of the examination system plays an important part in all these considerations. Litt says that the reform of study must essentially be a reform of examinations. The higher the number of students rises, the more estranged must examiners and examinees become, and the greater is the danger of concentrating only on knowledge of facts. Associated with this is the increase in the range of knowledge demanded for examinations, and this is not the least of the factors contributing to the internal crisis of university study.

The reform which is here necessary cannot be merely the unloading of historical and statistical ballast desiderated by certain schools of education—already outworn—which claimed to start from 'man himself'. It is all the more necessary to examine not only the candidate's knowledge of facts but also his understanding of the significance of his facts and his capacity for independent work. Under this heading it may seem a worth-while proposal to insert an intermediate examination either in the middle of the course, as is done already in medicine and chemistry, or still better to make more use of the exercises and seminars for the control of the students' work, so that the final verdict may rest on a broader basis than the isolated act of examination. But owing to the overwork of most lecturers such proposals are easier made than carried out.

In illustration of the problems of reform which are in the air to-day one may mention here the significant proposal made by E. Spranger in 1930 in his highly esteemed essay 'On the menace to and reform of the German university'.[1] As the result of a severe criticism of present conditions, and taking into consideration the broad middle stratum of educational requirements, Spranger demands that a study stage corresponding roughly to that of an American college should be incorporated in the university. This 'lower story', which would remain in direct contact with the 'upper story' of genuine scholarship, would have three functions: (1) to follow up school education; (2) to provide vocational training; (3) to give a synthetic view of civilization. The education given by this lower stage would suffice for all those students whose calling and inclination is not specifically scholastic, and would yet open to them 'a prospect of the wider relations in which the particular branches of study stand'. It is significant that a university teacher who stands in the foremost rank of the disciples and apostles of the German university idea should consider so extensive a reconstruction. In the main his plan fits into the tendency to grading already discussed. Whether the sharp division of all study into two parts, which is peculiar to Spranger's theory, has practical prospects, depends on the answer to two questions: Who shall remain restricted to the lower grade, and what professions will let themselves be confined to it? The general tendency to raise professional standards more and more and the academic pride among professional men in Germany must arouse fear at this point. There must also be serious doubt whether an organic union of 'upper and lower story' could be achieved. However, the discussion of Spranger's idea, the further realization of which would be of the highest interest, has only just begun.

To conclude this survey, two important *partial reforms* in

[1] E. Spranger, *Über Gefährdung und Erneuerung der deutschen Universität.*

the university system should be noticed, which are being carried out in 1932—reform of technical and reform of legal study.

The reform of the *technical colleges* has from the first had its particular problems, many of which are quite different from those of the universities (especially on their arts side) which we have delineated here. While the humanities now press, more strongly than medicine or natural science, for more systematization, in technical study it is just the other way; having been severely overburdened by a continuous increase in the number of lectures and examination courses, the demand is now for more academic freedom. The need here was great. The so-called general departments, whose main object is cultural, could up till now fulfil but imperfectly their function of rounding out the student's education, as he was overburdened with his own special subject. The technical college at Karlsruhe has now gone ahead with a reform: a considerable decrease in the number of obligatory lectures, a stressing of the general ideas that underlie all specialized studies. In this manner an effort is made towards a more fundamental study of individual subjects and at the same time towards securing more scope for general education. The humanistic motive, which has been powerfully active for years among technical students, and which has also inspired the so-called work-student both morally and socially, is plainly to be seen in this Karlsruhe reform, which will probably set an example for the rest of the technical colleges.

The Prussian State, after thorough consultation with experts and law faculties, introduced on July 1st, 1931, a reform of *legal study*. Here also the number of general lectures has been emphatically limited and an intensifying of study has been aimed at; certainly not through an extension of liberty, but on the contrary by stricter organization. Participation in the most important seminars is made dependent on an entrance certificate, normally acquired after three semesters, and a definite plan of study is prescribed. The introduction of discussion classes is also important, together with the increase in the number of seminars and the drawing in of legal practitioners to help in the training of students. The coaches, who hitherto had worked independently, outside the academic sphere, have now been drawn into the university. The number of participants in the exercises and coaching classes is limited in the interest of a stronger personal contact between teachers and students; to this end the State is appointing numerous new assistants. There is much criticism of these measures. The fear is general that university methods of study will be lowered to school level. Yet the reform of legal study, on which the legal and political development after 1918 has imposed new and extensive tasks, fulfils without doubt basic requirements of the present movement for reform. The newly organized legal faculty in Prussia will become an instructive experimental field for university reform in general.

Just before this article was concluded, a movement began, through the publication of a combined memorandum by the Universities' and Philologists' Associations, for reform in the training of *secondary school teachers*. This, as is rightly stressed, involves the reform of the central faculty of the university, that of philosophy. The programme is moderate. Scholarship remains the basis of professional training— scholarship in the specifically German form of combined research and teaching. With this, however, more attention is demanded for the pedagogical aspect of the course; more consciously than hitherto must the teacher be trained to teach. The new proposals for the course of study fall mostly under the head of examination reform; an organization of examinations that shall be 'more worthy and true to their inward purpose'! An elastic system of control in the seminars is to take the place of a formal intermediate examination. Philological study, too, is to be planned and graded to a moderate degree, and the assistant teaching staff to be added to, partly from the ranks of experienced teachers. The main ideas of this memorandum are identical with those behind the reform of the Prussian legal faculty. It is probable that they also will be sanctioned.

It is at the moment hard to see how far essential reforms are necessary in the remaining courses of study. The *theological* faculties of both confessions are now certainly passing through a significant change; the centre of gravity is shifting from the Historical to the Systematic and to the effort at adjustment to modern conditions. But they suffer less than other faculties, because the number of their students still keeps within relatively modest limits. The faculty of *medicine* has for a long time been considerably ahead of the other faculties in the improved systematization of instruction. Difficulties have arisen here from overcrowding, analogous to those of the technical colleges. The vital problems of medical study lie, however, distinctly on another plane. If, as seems likely, 'the whole man' becomes in future the subject of the doctor's art, then the emphasis and the general attitude of medical study will be considerably modified. But all these questions really play a secondary part at the present stage of university reform. At the moment we have principally to solve the problems of organization. Our first objective is, with a fundamentally conservative intent, to adapt academic instruction to the new situation which has been created by the overcrowding of the university and the transformation in the character of its students. We must remind ourselves at the same time, despite the fruitful and indispensable work that has been done, that even these present difficulties of the university are not to be overcome by organization alone. The process of perfecting the organization in itself demands from teachers and students

a more profound personal determination to achieve the
universitas.

. . . .

One would wish, in concluding this survey, to say a word
upon the *future* of the German university. But when one
contemplates this one feels immediately the oppressive ob-
scurity which at present veils all questions of the future of
Germany. We do well at the moment to give up planning
extensive cultural and political programmes for the German
university. More than ever are we compelled to distinguish
the desirable from the necessary. The necessity to-day and as
far as one can see into the future is a determined staving-off of
the acute dangers that threaten our whole conception of the
university, both through the overcrowding of students and
through the tendency to overdo school methods. The overcrowding to-day limits almost painfully the desire to make
the university a more profoundly organic part of the life of
the nation. The revolutionary manifestoes in which some
people at this critical time feel impelled to demand a fundamental reform of the academic world, must inevitably remain
scraps of paper.

That which is really essential for the preservation and development of the academic heritage will after all, when all
administrative reforms have been made, rest primarily in the
hands of the individual university teacher. Work done with
consciousness of responsibility and devotion to the demand
of the time, which is not the demand of the moment, is the
best and most vital piece of university reform. Even to-day,
at this time of general restriction, the way still lies open. The
German university will for certain not go under in the 'crisis
of learning'. The unrest and radicalism of discussion concerning the methods of learning, which makes anxious and
dogmatic natures so afraid, holds in itself the promise of a
fruitful issue, and there are signs among the students that this

promise is already being fulfilled, that the determination for a humanistic *universitas* is not yet dead even in the youngest generation. We cannot wait for a new uniform philosophy which might give back to the West that unity of *Weltanschauung* which seems irretrievably lost. More important and more sane than such dreamings is a fresh attempt to achieve a philosophical consciousness, a philosophical attitude in the individual branches of learning, which will then build an enduring bridge between professional study and humane education.

The German university of to-day does not lay claim to a monopoly in the education of the nation. It recognizes more clearly than ever that its way is not the only way to education. It can but desire and work to make this superstition disappear, and with it the academic pride of the German citizen which is twined around it. The more it disappears, the less those who want to rise in the social scale feel forced exclusively into channels of academic study, the more will the university be free to fulfil its essential mission. Let us rid ourselves of the harmful misconception that all intellectuals must be born 'leaders' of the nation and again that all leaders of the nation must be intellectuals. Do not let us overwhelm the university with an honour and a burden which are foreign to its character, by asking it to realize through the education it gives the ideals of the 'new man' or of the 'true German'. If it really ever was in a position for such an achievement it is not so to-day—and it has in truth no need to be ashamed of its limitations at a time which is everywhere resounding with high demands and is scarce anywhere capable of realizing them. It is by conforming to this very sober recognition of its limitations that the university acquires the right and the prospect of exercising to the full its most sovereign duty as the guardian of pure knowledge in these times of fanaticism and of faith in the doctrine of might. Come what may, we cannot and will not think of the future of Europe without this watcher and guardian of the intellect. Greater forces must and will 'make' history. But only interpreted history is true human history. Precisely in order that we may not be engulfed in chaos, but remain on the route of true human history, the university remains a necessity of life for Germany and for Europe.

Universities in Great Britain[1]

By ERNEST BARKER, LL.D.

(Professor of Political Science in the University of Cambridge.)

The Purposes, Government, and Areas of British Universities

WE may define a university, in British theory and practice, as an organized and degree-giving institution, intended for the study and advancement of higher branches of learning, self-governing in its nature, and, to a greater or less extent, national in its scope. Three questions arise from this definition. They relate to the intention, the government, and the scope of British universities.

The *intention*, though it has just been stated in a single phrase ('the study and the advancement of the higher branches of learning'), is really twofold. The aim of a university is, in the first place, to give the highest and final stage of general education to undergraduate students between the age of 18 and that of 22, partly with a view to preparing them for a specific profession or calling (such as that of engineering or again of medicine), but partly, and still more, with a view to preparing them for doing work of a better quality, in virtue of the better training they have received, in *any* profession or calling which they may subsequently enter. A university fulfils this first aim not only through the intellectual

[1] This article, with minor differences, has been published in book form by the Student Christian Movement Press on behalf of International Student Service. The editors wish to acknowledge the courtesy of that publishing firm in allowing it to be reprinted here.

equipment which it provides, but also through the moral quality of the common life which its existence brings into play—a common life of residence, issuing in various forms of spontaneous social activity, which serves as a discipline and a stimulus to all upon whom it acts. The double design of 'forming and strengthening the character' as well as of 'developing the intelligence' pervades English education from the elementary school to the university.

The second aim of a university is to promote and conduct research in the humanities and the various branches of science, partly through its professors and lecturers, and partly through the graduate students whom it attracts; and this with a view both to increasing the sum of human knowledge and to deepening the current of human thought, so that a university may thus serve the national community in which it is set (and so far as possible the world at large) as a leader and guide in the fields of theology and philosophy, letters and history, politics and economics, science (both pure and applied), and the other interests and activities of the human mind. Until the middle of the nineteenth century it may be said that this office was mainly discharged by our British universities in the fields of theology and classical studies. Since the latter half of the nineteenth century the universities have been drawn, or have moved, into 'fresh woods and pastures new'; but they have not forgotten their ancient interests.

Finally, and by way of a corollary, or as a by-product, of this second aim, it has also become a purpose of our universities to disseminate knowledge and the spirit of true learning among the general public outside their walls. This extra-mural activity may take the form of providing, even within the university itself, a system of free 'public' lectures: it may take the form of giving, in different local centres, 'Extension' lectures and courses for those who desire such forms of instruction; it may take the form of providing 'tutorial' classes, with a tutorial form of instruction, for workers in towns and even in villages. The system of 'extension' lectures has now been established for fifty years: the system of 'tutorial' classes dates back nearly twenty-five years.

The *government* of British universities is, in the main, a system of government by university teachers. The finances of the university are administered, its courses are planned, and the appointments of its teachers are made by the university itself. There is indeed a distinction, in this respect, between the 'old' universities of Oxford and Cambridge and the 'new' universities of England and Wales together with the Scottish universities. The universities of Oxford and Cambridge are entirely governed by teachers. The 'new' universities and the Scottish universities are governed in the main by a body (a 'Council', or, as it is called in Scotland, a 'Court') on which persons drawn from outside the university sit side by side with the representatives of its teachers. But in both sorts of universities the teachers are the mainspring of university policy; and both sorts of universities are remarkably free from control by the State.

The State, it is true, touches the universities; and it touches them in three ways. In the first place, apart from the old universities, which simply grew without any warrant, it is the State which, through the Privy Council, gives the universities their charter and authorizes them to confer their degrees. In the second place, the Government has the executive power of appointing a 'royal commission' of inquiry to report upon any university; and Parliament may then, by legislative act, appoint a 'statutory commission' to make statutes for a university in general accordance with the findings of such a report. Actually, however, a royal commission will only be appointed, as a rule, when there is already a strong demand from within in favour of some reform: it will usually contain several members drawn from the university concerned; the same will be equally or even more true of a statutory commission; and a statutory commission will also consult the university authorities in framing its statutes. Finally, the State makes annual contributions on a considerable scale to the incomes of all the British universities, including Oxford and Cambridge: the modest subsidy of £15,000, voted by Parliament in 1889, has now grown to £1,800,000. It might have been expected that an increase in financial contribution would have been accompanied by an increase in financial control; but this has not actually been the result. The body on whose recommendations the contribution of the State is allocated to the different universities is a standing committee of the Treasury (not of the Board of Education), and this committee is composed of persons possessing a wide academic experience, in complete sympathy with the universities, in which they all have been students and most of them teachers, and firmly believing in the general principle of university autonomy. Further, it is the policy of the committee to make 'block' grants to universities, without any specification or control of the objects upon which such grants may be spent. The State thus leaves British universities remarkably free at the same time that it helps them in their work.

The *scope* of British universities—that is to say, the territorial area which they cover, and from which they draw their students—was described in our preliminary definition as being 'to a greater or less extent national'. This is a description which needs some explanation. All the universities draw students from the whole of Great Britain, and indeed from the Empire at large. The University of Leeds, for example, may have medical students drawn not only from Northern, but also from Southern England, and in addition from some of the Dominions; and the University of London will draw its medical students from an even greater area. Engineering students will similarly come from all quarters to the different universities, sometimes (it may be) led by chance, and sometimes attracted by a particular speciality, to the university which they prefer. Post-graduate students, again, who have already taken an undergraduate course at some university, may move to any of the British universities for a further course of research; and this class includes a large number of overseas students who have come from the Empire at large. But there is a distinction to be drawn, none the less, in this matter of scope or territorial area, between the old universities of Oxford and Cambridge and the newer universities of England and Wales.

The old universities have no limit of territorial area and no particular local connexion. They draw indifferently on the nation at large. The newer universities, even if they have some of the ramifications which have just been described, are nevertheless on the whole and in the main 'provincial' or 'civic' universities. They draw their students in the arts and sciences, and also, to a large extent, in medicine and engineering, from the particular region or city in which they are placed and with which they are particularly connected.[1] This distinction between the old and the newer universities is mainly the product of historical development. The old universities had existed for nearly seven centuries before the newer universities came into the field. They had established a national position: they had accumulated a national prestige. History, which has created their position and prestige, may create changes and modifications. Meanwhile we may notice in passing (as we shall have occasion to notice again) that the

[1] The Scottish universities, in this respect, stand somewhat apart. They are all, as we shall see, 'old' universities: they are all, to some extent, the 'national' universities of Scotland. But each of them tends to be connected with a particular area of Scotland; and they thus approximate to the new universities of England and Wales.

regional connexion of the newer universities, if it limits their scope, also gives them a regional root, a regional support, and a regional influence which invigorate their life and strengthen their hold.

Undergraduate Courses, 'Honours' and 'Pass'

In all the British universities there is a distinction between an 'Honours' and a 'Pass' form of the undergraduate course, which involves a corresponding distinction between an 'Honours' and a 'Pass' (or 'Ordinary') form of the Bachelor's degree taken at the end of the course. The 'Honours' Course, as its name suggests, is more intensive and more thorough; and it culminates, at the end of the three (sometimes four) years' period of study, in a written examination, extending over five or even six days, in which the student's proficiency and knowledge are thoroughly tested. The quality of the Honours—First, Second, or Third—attained in this written examination is generally a fair indication of a student's general ability and indeed of his future career. In the University of Cambridge there are some fourteen of these Honours Courses (in classics, history, philosophy, natural sciences, economics, theology, law, and a number of other subjects); and each course is managed by a Committee, or Board, of the teachers concerned. In both of the two old universities, and in the University of London, an Honours Course is taken by the great majority of the students; and the tendency is running in that direction in most of the British universities.[1]

The Pass (or Ordinary) Course is more composite in its

---

[1] In England, 4,027 students took Honours Degrees in the last year for which records are available, and 2,048 took Pass Degrees. In Wales the figures were 272 and 248. In Scotland the order is reversed, and while the number of Pass Degrees was 1,571, the number of Honours Degrees was only 499. The Honours system is more recent in Scotland, and there is still a large vogue of the 'Ordinary' course.

character, including a number of different subjects; the examinations involved are generally spread over the course; and the work of the student is naturally less intense and less concentrated. Indeed it is perhaps a just criticism, in regard to the two old universities, that the Pass Course is too shallow and too diffuse. Such a criticism, however, could not justly be directed against the Pass Courses of the newer and the Scottish universities. Here the subjects of the Pass Courses, and the lectures in each subject, are carefully planned; and a Pass Course followed under such conditions may be a better preparation for a student who intends to be a teacher, either in a primary or a secondary school, than a highly specialized Honours Course in a single subject such as Chemistry.

Post-Graduate Work

The great majority of students go no farther than the undergraduate course, just as the great majority of medieval students never went beyond the *Trivium* and the *Quadrivium* of the Arts course. Post-graduate work has assumed no large dimensions in the British universities. In those universities in which a separate test, involving a dissertation, is required for a Master's degree, a certain amount of more or less advanced study is encouraged by the requirement. But advanced study of a regular and definitely post-graduate character is mainly connected with the new degree of *Philosophiae Doctor*, which was instituted by the British universities about a dozen years ago, towards the end of the War. The degree was intended to attract American students: it has actually attracted British, Indian, and a certain number of Dominion students. It involves, as a rule, three years of graduate work under the guidance of a supervisor; and the object of the work is the production of a thesis containing an original contribution to knowledge. In the departments of natural science the system of supervision is probably active and effective. The common life of a scientific laboratory spontaneously provides incentive and direction for work of research. In the various departments of the humanities little has yet been done to organize seminars or to provide courses of advanced lectures. This distinction is perhaps reflected in the distribution of advanced students between natural science, pure and applied, and the various branches of the humanities.[1] Of some 2,100 full-time advanced students recorded for the academic year 1928–9, 800 only were working in what may be called arts subjects (150, for instance, in history, 120 in English, and 110 in economics and politics): the remaining 1,300 were engaged either in purely scientific subjects (450 in chemistry and 180 in physics) or in various subjects of applied science, such as medicine, engineering, and agriculture. It may be added that the total number of full-time students in British universities is something over 44,000. The ratio of advanced undergraduate students is thus 1 to 21, and advanced students are less than 5 per cent. of the total number of students.

University Teachers, Finances, and Equipment

The teachers of British universities fall into four main grades. In the first grade, that of the Professoriate, there are about 750 persons, each with an average salary of nearly £1,100. In the second, that of Readers, Assistant Professors,

[1] There is, however, an economic reason for the larger proportion of research students in the various subjects of natural science. The bulk of the students who have taken a first degree in arts tend to enter immediately into the teaching profession; and on the other hand students who have taken a first degree in natural science are encouraged, and sometimes required, by industrial firms to engage in research, and to proceed to a higher degree, before they are given employment as technical specialists. It should also be added that post-graduate or research studentships (such as those awarded by the State Department of Scientific and Industrial Research) go largely to students of natural science.

and Independent Lecturers, there are 315 persons, each with an average salary of about £630. The other two grades are those of Lecturers, and of Assistant Lecturers and Demonstrators in Laboratories. Apart from the two old universities, which have a system of their own for these last two grades, there are about 1,050 Lecturers, with an average salary of £460, and 775 Assistant Lecturers and Demonstrators with average salaries of £310. The tenure of the teaching posts, in the higher grades, is 'up to the age fixed for retirement'; and that age is generally 65. The system of ascending grades makes it a comparatively simple matter (simple, at any rate, in comparison with the difficulties in German universities) for a young graduate student of ability to find a post in the service of a university.

The estimation of university teachers in general national opinion may be said to stand high. It has grown with the growth of the universities, and it has grown amazingly. One of the features of the intellectual life of Great Britain, even as late as the middle of the reign of Queen Victoria, was the predominance of the amateur. It was not the professional professor, but the private scholar, who made our learning and our culture. Our historians were men such as Grote and Macaulay; our philosophers were men such as Mill and Spencer; our economists were men such as Ricardo and Bagehot; and many even of our scientists, such as Darwin and A. R. Wallace, lived and worked outside the universities. We have changed all that. The position is now reversed: as learning has become more specialized, it has also become more professionalized: the universities and their teachers are ousting, or have ousted, the amateur; and it is they who nowadays dominate the general field of learning. The change was inevitable; but perhaps it has not been, in all respects, a change for the better. The professional historian may be more thorough than the amateur, but he may also have less contact with national life, and less understanding of its problems; the philosopher of the universities, if he is more learned, may also be more scholastic. One of the great duties of the university teacher is to remain a man in becoming a scholar, and to keep a rich humanity at the same time that he acquires a large erudition.

Bacon, when he wrote of universities in his *Advancement of Learning*, desired more abundant endowment and equipment. The British universities cannot in these matters vie with the American; but they have made great advances in the course of this century. Their total income is now £5,000,000 per annum. Nearly a half of this amount is provided from public funds. The State itself, partly through its University Grants Committee and partly through other channels, provides 36 per cent. of the whole: the Local Authorities provide a further 10 per cent. A little less than a third (31 per cent.) arises from the fees paid by students for matriculation, tuition, examinations, and graduation. The remaining 23 per cent. of the income of the universities is mainly drawn from endowments, donations, and subscriptions, which amount to a little over 16 per cent. of the whole.

We do not do justice, however, to the extent of private generosity if we confine our attention to the part which it plays in providing annual income. We have also to take into account the amount of capital gifts. Such capital gifts, largely due to the generosity of private benefactors, are almost entirely responsible for the provision of new buildings. It is not the State grant, but the private benefactor, the voluntary donations made in answer to appeals, and the grants of charitable and educational trusts, which explain the expansion of the laboratories, the lecture halls, and the general accommodation of British universities.

In the matter of buildings there is a contrast—produced

by the past, very striking in the present, but likely to be modified and softened in the future—between the architecture, the amenities, and the general surroundings of the two old universities, and those of almost all the rest. Oxford and Cambridge have profited by the piety and the munificence of medieval bishops, royal patrons, and noble benefactors: the one can still show medieval enchantments; the other, in some of its colleges, still shows a solemn Tudor splendour. Both have green lawns, aspiring towers, great courts, and quadrangles,

Fluminaque antiquos subterlabentia muros.

The other universities are mostly set on urban sites: the bustle of streets encompasses their life; and their buildings are sometimes hardly distinguishable from the offices and edifices by which they are surrounded. But a change is already beginning to stir; and the next fifty years may greatly alter, if they cannot abolish, the existing contrast. The University of London has recently acquired a site in Bloomsbury, behind the British Museum, on which it is planning the erection of a central block of buildings: the University of Bristol has recently erected not only a great Physical Laboratory, but also a noble tower, with an adjacent hall and library, not unworthy of the Middle Ages; and the University of Birmingham is planning a 'campus' on the American model.

One of the glories of British universities, as it is also their peculiarity and distinction among the universities of the world, is the University Presses of Oxford and Cambridge. They are both ancient: the Press at Oxford goes back to 1468, and Cambridge was printing books as long ago as 1521. The privilege of printing copies of the Bible and the Book of Common Prayer, which they share with the King's Printer, was perhaps in the past the basis of their strength; and on this basis they were able to undertake the unremunerative publication of learned works on a far greater scale than any other publishing concern. The Clarendon Press has published the *Oxford English Dictionary*; it is publishing a new edition of a great Greek Lexicon; it owns, and is bringing up to date, the *Dictionary of National Biography*; and its editions of Biblical and classical texts are known to all scholars. While Oxford has thus turned more particularly to Dictionaries and texts, Cambridge of late years has turned to collective histories: it has published, or is publishing, a Cambridge Ancient, a Cambridge Medieval, and a Cambridge Modern History; and in the same way it has published, or is publishing, Cambridge Histories of English Literature, of British Foreign Policy, of the British Empire and of India. Both universities, besides publishing works of learning and scholarship, have also published works of general literature, and that in a form and a style of printing which perhaps no ordinary firm of publishers can equal; and both have aided the general development of education, not only in universities but also in schools, by the series of text-books which they have issued.

The libraries of the old universities, no less than their printing presses, are among their glories. The Bodleian Library at Oxford and the University Library at Cambridge are both national institutions. In the range which they cover, and the number of volumes which they contain, they stand by the side of the British Museum. Like the British Museum, and along with the National Libraries of Scotland and Wales, they enjoy the benefits of the Copyright Act, and are entitled to receive copies of all works which are published in Great Britain.

It must be confessed that a certain tendency towards technological specialization has invaded British universities, as it has also invaded many American and some continental universities. Brewing has made its appearance in the University of Birmingham; and the study of Textiles, aided by a large equipment, is prosecuted in the University of Leeds. The University of London has a School of Journalism: in common with the Universities of Birmingham and Manchester, it has a Faculty of Commerce and awards a Commerce Degree; and proposals for 'Schools of Business Administration' are being canvassed in other universities. A more healthy form of this general movement is the special researches in various problems of Applied Science which are now being conducted in a number of universities. These researches have generally been inspired, and they are generally aided, by Departments of Government such as the Department of Scientific and Industrial Research, the Medical Research Council, the Ministry of Agriculture, and the Empire Marketing Board.

Co-operation between the British universities has largely increased during the last dozen years. Like most institutions in this country (perhaps, indeed, like most human institutions), they showed in the past an individualism which, if it has not disappeared, has lost some of its angularity. There is now a University Bureau of the British Empire, with offices in London; there is a Vice-Chancellors' Committee, representing the different universities of Great Britain, which meets regularly at these offices; there is an Annual Conference of the Universities of Great Britain; and there is a Quinquennial Congress of the Universities of the Empire.

Students: their Studies and their Sports

The degree of university supervision of a student's work naturally varies from place to place. It is, as we shall see later, one thing in the older universities, and another thing in the newer and the Scottish universities. Generally, however, it may be said that the British system, so far as there is

3937   H

a system, is a *via media* between the system of the United States and that of Germany. There are no 'assignations', no 'quizzes', no regular 'checking up', as in the American universities: there is no gradual passage to a degree by the accumulation of 'credits' on the strength of serial examinations conducted by a Professor at the end of each semester. Under the 'Honours' system the student 'reads', largely by himself, for a final examination which generally comes at the end of his three years' course and is conducted with the aid of external examiners. On the other hand, there is much more guidance and supervision of a student's work than is generally given in German universities. The undergraduate knows his teachers personally and receives personal instruction from them; and the system of 'tuition', which is spreading from the older universities to the rest, ensures that element of personal contact and intercourse between teacher and taught which is generally regarded by British opinion as essential to true education. In one respect, however, the British student profits less by his opportunities than the student of the German universities. The migration of a student from one university to another, during his undergraduate stage, is almost unknown; and it is still rare, even at the graduate stage, for a student to migrate to another university and to get the benefit of a new environment and a new inspiration.

Sport is a prominent feature in all British universities, and especially at Oxford and Cambridge. Sometimes it encroaches on the domain of work; but in all its manifestations, which take the form of contests between organized teams, it serves as an outlet of corporate sense and a channel of university feeling. In this respect the British universities are not unlike the American. On the other hand, all forms of sport are entirely managed by the students themselves; and there is only one university which assigns any member of its staff to organize or even to encourage the sports of its students. So far as there is 'coaching', it is voluntarily given by old members of the university: the equipment is modest, the 'gates' are small, and no 'big money' is received or paid. At the same time the general public has a deep interest in the sports of the old universities; and it shares the general Anglo-Saxon tendency to value educational institutions in terms of their athletic eminence.

Besides their full-time students, many of the universities include a number of part-time students. Most of these students are men (or women) who are engaged in work during the day, and can only attend the university in the evening. Such 'evening students' (as they are often described) are particularly numerous in the University of London, where many of them take regular courses and succeed in gaining a regular degree.

Not only do the universities seek to make provision for students who are already engaged in work; they seek to provide work and to find employment for their students on the completion of their courses. 'Appointments Boards' are maintained by many of the universities; and through these Boards students are often enabled to find posts, not only in the field of education, but also in that of commerce and industry. Particularly in this latter way these Boards are widening the area of opportunity for university graduates; and at the same time, and by the same process, they are building a bridge between the university and the world of business.

Mention has already been made, in the beginning of this chapter, of a common life of residence as issuing in various forms of spontaneous social activity. England is a country of 'clubs'; and its universities are over full of students' clubs—the more so, in proportion as the universities are more definitely residential. In the two old universities the two most famous clubs are the Oxford and Cambridge Unions—both about a century old; both formed for purposes of debate, in parliamentary form, which often reaches a high level, and both possessing their own premises, with a debating hall, a library, a newspaper-room, and other amenities. The two old universities have also a variety of other University Societies—dramatic societies, which produce English and sometimes Greek plays; musical societies; political societies, either party or non-party; and a rich crop of other groups, from 'film guilds' and poetry clubs to vigorous branches of the League of Nations Union and economic societies. In addition to the university societies there are also the college societies or clubs—debating, musical, historical, classical— where subjects are discussed, or music played, or papers read. It is all managed by students themselves; it is all a real and essential part of their development. In the 'new' and the Scottish universities the organization of students' clubs is somewhat different. Generally there is a comprehensive Union Society, including all the students of the university, and further including a sort of federation, the various particular student clubs—athletic, debating, dramatic, and the like. These 'Union Societies' are thus general and powerful bodies: their 'president' plays a large part in general student life: he will be in close touch, again and again, with the official authorities of his university; and he will also be in contact, from time to time, with the student organizations of other colleges.

On this basis has arisen, since the War, the National Union of Students in England and Wales—a general centre for co-operation between the students of different universities, corresponding, in its way, to the official organs of co-operation between the authorities of different universities mentioned at the end of the previous section. The National Union is mainly pivoted on the 'Union Societies' of the newer universities, though it is also connected with the 'Unions' of the two old universities. It interests itself in questions of common concern to all students—the provision of hostels, arrangement for foreign travel, and the like—as well as in the promotion of intercourse between students of different universities. Two other general organizations of British students must also be mentioned. One is the Student Christian Movement of Great Britain and Ireland, with some 12,000 members, mainly drawn from universities; the other is the British Universities League of Nations Society, which draws together the various university societies devoted to the cause of internationalism.

Geographical Distribution of British Universities

We may now pass to consider the distribution of universities and university students among the three parts of Great Britain—Scotland, Wales, and England.[1]

In Scotland there are four universities. Three of them were papally founded (according to the practice of the later Middle Ages) in the course of the fifteenth century: the fourth (Edinburgh) was founded by the Town Council of Edinburgh towards the close of the sixteenth century. There are about 11,000 students in these four universities. The population of Scotland at the time of the last census was a little short of 5,000,000. It follows that the student population of Scotland is to the total population as 1 to 455.

In Wales there is a single university. The university,

[1] Politically, the unit of British government is Great Britain and Northern Ireland; and mention should therefore be made of the University of Northern Ireland—the Queen's University of Belfast, which dates, in its present form, from 1909. Northern Ireland, however, has had a parliament of its own since 1922; and its university, while it is connected in many ways with the British universities (it continues, for example, to send a representative to the British Parliament), belongs, in the main, to a different system.

which is a federal university, dates only from the year 1893;
but the four colleges of which it is composed are (with one
exception) of a slightly earlier date. The number of students
in the University of Wales is 2,660. The population of Wales
at the last census (including Monmouthshire) was 2,650,000.
The student population of Wales is thus to the total population of the country as 1 to 1,000.

In England there are eleven universities. They fall
historically into three groups. (1) Two of them, the two
'old' Universities of Oxford and Cambridge, belong to the
earlier part of the Middle Ages. We may assign the beginnings of Oxford to the period about 1167, when Henry II
recalled English students from Paris in the course of his
quarrel with Becket: we may attribute the origin of Cambridge (which in its beginnings was something in the nature
of a colony) to the period about 1209, when a migration took
place from Oxford to Cambridge in consequence of a dispute
between the University and the Town of Oxford. (2) Two
of the other English universities, Durham and London,
belong to the period of the Reform Bill, which in this respect,
as in so many others, marks a great 'divide' in English
History. Durham was founded in 1832, and London in 1836,
but two of the constituent colleges of the University of
London (University College and King's College) are of a
slightly earlier date than the University.[1] (3) The other seven
universities of England, in their present form, belong to the
twentieth century; but the first beginnings of many of them

---

[1] University College was founded in 1826. It was originally intended
to be, but failed to become, a university. It was founded by Whigs and
Radicals, who objected, with great justice, to the predominantly clerical
and Tory complexion of the two old universities. Its foundation is thus
a great turning-point in the history of British universities—the more so
because, in addition to opening its doors to all creeds and parties, it also
sought to extend its curriculum to take in all subjects, including modern
science and modern languages.

go farther back, and in Manchester, for instance, university instruction is as old as 1850. Of these seven universities, two are in Lancashire (Manchester and Liverpool); two are in Yorkshire (Sheffield and Leeds); one is in the Midlands (Birmingham); one is in the south-west (Bristol); and one (Reading) is in the south. The whole student population of England (as it is given in the last return of the University Grants Committee, which, however, for technical reasons is not entirely complete) is nearly 31,000. The population of England at the last census was $35\frac{1}{4}$ millions. The student population is thus to the total population as 1 to 1,150.

The Problem of the Optimum University Population in Great Britain

We have seen that the student population of Scotland is 1 in 455 of the total population, and that of England 1 in 1,150. It follows that Scotland, in proportion to its total population, has five students where England has two. The difference may be explained partly by the Scottish tradition of a national zest for higher education, and partly by the superior advantages which are offered to poor students in Scotland and the lower fees of the Scottish universities. But Scotland itself cannot carry, or absorb, the whole of its own university product; and it is compelled to export, as it were, its surplus. This is successfully managed; but the figures which have just been cited none the less raise a large general question, over which we may pause for a moment.

What is the *optimum* amount of the university population of a country in proportion to its total population? Scotland, we have seen, answers 1 in 455; England answers 1 in 1,150. Germany, with its thirty universities and 90,000 students, answers 1 in 690; the United States answers (if we include all students in colleges, universities, and professional schools reporting to the federal Bureau of Education) 1 in 125. We must allow that the meaning of a university, and the significance of a university course, vary from country to country. Many of those who are classed as university students in the United States might not be classed in the same category either in Great Britain or in Germany. But the general problem still remains. It is obvious that too large a university population—a population largely exceeding the *optimum* number—may produce two bad results. It may congest the universities; it may reduce their system of instruction to a system of mechanical mass-production; it may lower their standard of examination to the standard of mere mechanical attainment. (It is already possible, in a British university, for a professor to find over 1,000 students taking the same course of lectures in his department.) Again, it may tend to produce an unemployed, or uncongenially and inadequately employed, intellectual proletariat; and an intellectual proletariat is the seed-bed of revolutionary movements, political and economic.

The problem can only be mentioned: its solution is a matter for each country, and it must vary from country to country. Two tentative remarks may, however, be made. The first is that, for England, our present proportion (1 in 1,150) is perhaps as much as we can safely attempt at the present time. It has, indeed, been suggested that every teacher in an elementary school should properly be a university graduate. This might double at a stroke our existing university population; and its general results—certainly in the universities, and possibly also the elementary schools themselves—might be serious. The second remark is that, under our English conditions, a university which is not a university of colleges—in other words a university which is not a decentralized or federal university—should not ideally exceed the number of 2,000 students. Otherwise it may tend to the machinery of mere organization, and it may lose the one thing needful—personal and individual contact between teachers and taught.

The Selection of University Students

What has just been said naturally raises the question of the selection of university students. If, as in England, a comparatively small proportion of the whole population can gain access to the university, that proportion ought to be carefully chosen; it ought to contain the spring of the year and the best intellectual promise of the nation; the process of admission to the university ought to be a process which ensures *la carrière ouverte aux talents*, wheresoever, and in whatever rank of society, talents are to be found. The British universities, like other universities, require of all candidates for admission the passing of an entrance (or 'Matriculation') examination. Some element of 'selection of the fittest' enters in this way. But there are two other elements which are much more important.

In the first place, and so far as concerns those universities which are universities of colleges, a further test is imposed by the college, in addition to that of the university, as a necessary condition of entry. In the two old universities in particular (which are both universities of colleges), the college authorities are confronted by a much larger number of applicants for admission than they can possibly accept; and both by examination and by personal interview they take pains to select the best of the applicants.

In the second place (and this is one of the most important features of the British system), there are a large number of scholarships and bursaries, tenable at the universities, which are awarded on the result of special and competitive examinations, and are generally given to poor and promising students. In some universities, indeed, such scholarships are open to all, both rich and poor; but even in these universities the *full* emoluments of a Scholarship are awarded only to those who are actually in need of assistance. The colleges of Oxford and Cambridge award about 450 Scholarships and other grants every year; and other universities make similar awards. This is not all. The State, through the Board of Education, grants 'State Scholarships' and other modes of assistance; the Local Education Authorities grant local (or 'county') scholarships; and public educational Charities (such as the Carnegie Trust for the Universities of Scotland) give various forms of aid which enable poor students of promise to proceed to the university. It has been calculated, on the basis of official returns, that nearly *one-half* of the total number of students in British universities have obtained assistance in one or other of these ways, on account of the promise they show, either before entering on a university career, or at some point in its course.[1]

This is a most important fact. It proves, in the first place, that British universities are in no way confined to any social section of the community; and it illustrates the British conception of a proper system of relations between higher education and what is called 'Democracy'. The Universities of Oxford and Cambridge, too often supposed to be the homes of the rich (and even of the 'idle rich'), contain 38·2 per cent. of assisted students—a figure which is only 2·4 below that for English universities at large. In the second place we are able to understand, in the light of this fact, the general British conception of the relation between the university and the community. It is a conception according to which the university, recruiting from every possible quarter,

[1] The actual percentages are—for England, 40·6; for Wales, 67·3; for Scotland, 52·7. The percentage for all the students of British universities is, according to the returns, 45·2; but as the returns are probably incomplete, the actual percentage may well be 50.

and drawing from the whole community, furnishes in turn to the community the trained men and the women who are likely to serve it best—the political leaders and the civil servants of the State, alike in local and in central government;[1] the members of the great professions, and particularly, perhaps, of the great profession of teaching; the men who direct commerce and industry, or provide them both with that managerial and technical skill which, with the increasing complexity of the economic world, they increasingly require for their service. There is an old prayer which is recited by the preacher in our old universities: 'That there never may be wanting a supply of persons duly qualified to serve God both in Church and State, let us pray for a blessing on all seminaries of sound learning and religious education.' It is a prayer which still inspires the practice of our universities. And the fact that British universities render this service to the State may perhaps be pleaded as the chief justification of that peculiar British anomaly (which like many British anomalies works tolerably in practice) whereby they are turned into constituencies—peculiar constituencies, lying somewhere between the territorial and the occupational—and are allowed, as such, to send some dozen members to the House of Commons.[2]

---

[1] In local government, it must be confessed, the universities have not yet begun to furnish any large proportion of the personnel. The problem of the proper recruitment of what may be called the 'local civil service' has still to be solved. But the education officers (or 'directors of education') who administer the ranges of education controlled by the more important Local Education Authorities are beginning to be drawn increasingly from the universities.

[2] It was James I who first made Oxford and Cambridge into parliamentary 'boroughs', each returning two 'burgesses'. The later nineteenth and the twentieth century have added further a member for London, two members for the 'combined' English universities, a member for Wales, and three members for the four universities of Scotland. A twelfth member represents the Queen's University of Belfast.

Universities and 'Secondary' Schools

There is one particular aspect of the relation of British universities to the community which deserves some mention in passing. It concerns the relation of the universities to the schools of the country, and particularly to what are generically called the 'secondary' schools—the schools in which children are taught from the age of 11 to that of 18 or 19, and which feed the universities. These schools (apart from private and voluntary foundations such as Eton and Harrow, Winchester and Rugby, which are called in England by the familiar, but to foreign observers perplexing, name of 'public schools') are mainly managed by Local Education Authorities with the aid and under the inspection of the State.[1] But the universities, in various ways, affect to a great degree the character and the curriculum of all 'secondary' education. They furnish the teachers; and both by their matriculation examination and by the examinations they conduct for the scholarships which they award they influence the courses. Nor is this all. The universities are examining bodies for all these schools. They conduct the examinations for 'certificates': they prescribe the curriculum on which these 'certificates' are awarded. These certificates—the School Certificate awarded at the age of 16, and the Higher Certificate awarded at the age of 18—are in the nature of passports into a career for those (and they are the great majority) who do not proceed to the university. In controlling this system of 'passports' the university plays a considerable part in the general scheme of national education.

Classification of the Main Groups of British Universities

Numerically, we may divide British universities into four

---

[1] Of 1,350 of these schools on the grant list of the Board of Education in 1929, 698 were controlled by Local Education Authorities, and 440 were endowed schools, many of them aided by those Authorities.

groups, each roughly equal in size to the others. There is the Scottish group, with 11,000 students, forming a quarter of the whole. There is the group (if two can be said to make a group) of the old universities of England, with 10,200 students, forming another quarter. There are the various institutions of the University of London, with 9,150 internal students,[1] forming a third and smaller quarter. Finally, there are the newer 'provincial' or 'civic' universities of England and Wales, with nearly 14,000 students, forming the last and the largest of the four groups.

While, however, we may thus distinguish four numerical or quantitative groups, it is possible, and it is preferable, in seeking to understand the character of British universities, to reduce the number of groups to two. One of these will be the old universities of Oxford and Cambridge. The other will be the new universities which have arisen in England and Wales in the last century, together with the Scottish universities. It is true, indeed, that the Scottish universities have a considerable antiquity. St. Andrews, the oldest, is as old as 1411: Edinburgh, the youngest, is no more recent than 1582. None the less, as we shall see, the Scottish universities have some essential affinities with the newer universities of England and Wales.

The Old Universities of Oxford and Cambridge

The two old universities are peculiar in several respects.[2]

[1] There are also a large number of 'external' students of the University of London who can sit for examinations, and take degrees, in the University, without attending at any of its lectures or in any of its laboratories. It should be noticed, and it is an important fact, that the University has now begun to attempt to provide advice and guidance for these students in their reading.

[2] Oxford and Cambridge are here treated together; but they differ, of course, from one another in many respects. Three may be mentioned. (1) In the distribution of their students among subjects of study, Oxford inclines more to the subjects of the faculty of arts, and Cambridge inclines

Not only are they more ancient; they are also, as we have already had reason to notice, more national in their scope, and they draw their students more widely and more indifferently from every part of Great Britain. They have also a more residential character. In the newer and the Scottish universities the great bulk of the students are 'day' students: they live at home, and they come to the university, by train or otherwise, for daily instruction. Some of the students, it is true, live in university hostels (10 per cent. of the men students and over 25 per cent. of the women); and all the students participate in a lively round of student activities (sports and debates, dances and dramatic performances) conducted on the university grounds or in the university buildings. None the less, the fact remains that over half

more to the subjects of pure and applied science. Including both men and women, we find that Oxford has 3,800 students in arts (83·5), and a little over 750 (of whom over 500 are students of pure science) in all other subjects (16·5); while Cambridge has 3,325 students (58·8) in arts, and 2,330 (of whom nearly 1,200 are students of pure science, 580 are students of technology, and over 380 are students of medicine) in all other subjects (41·2). (2) The proportion of candidates for Honours is greater in Oxford than in Cambridge. If we limit our attention to men (there is a tradition that the women students in the two old universities shall only take Honours), we find that in Oxford, according to the last returns, 696 men took Honours Degrees in the year of reckoning, and 137 took Pass Degrees: in Cambridge 923 men took Honours Degrees in the same year, and 533 took Pass Degrees. In the one, about 20 men took Honours Degrees for 4 who took Pass Degrees: in the other, 7 men took Honours Degrees for 4 who took Pass Degrees. Peculiar conditions in Cambridge (e.g. the larger number of students who take a serious pass course in Engineering, and the larger proportion of medical students who take a general pass course at the same time that they follow the study of medicine) go some way to explain the difference. (3) The proportion of students (again counting men only) who reside in a college is greater in Oxford than in Cambridge. In the former, of 3,730 men, 2,090 reside in college and 1,640 in rooms or lodgings outside: in the latter, of 5,170 men, 2,020 reside in college and 3,150 outside. The proportion in college is 56 per cent. in the former, and 39 per cent. in the latter. But figures such as these can only give, at the best, a very imperfect idea of the differences between Oxford and Cambridge.

(54·5 per cent.) of the students of the newer and the Scottish universities live at home; and a large majority of the remainder live scattered in lodgings over large urban areas. The students of Oxford and Cambridge are almost all living at a distance from their homes; and they reside either in colleges, or in contiguous lodgings packed closely together in towns of which each has a population of only some 60,000. This permits, and indeed encourages, the growth of a common student life (over and above the official life of the university), with a quality of its own and a crop of spontaneous activities sufficient to fill nearly twenty-four hours of the day. Under these conditions a second education develops—the education of students by themselves—which some have held to be the greater education of the two.[1] It would be a mistake to think that the second education does not also exist in the day universities. It would also be a mistake to think that it exists, or can possibly exist, to the same extent.

The essential unit of residence in the old universities is the college. But the college is not only a unit of residence. It is also a unit of education; for each college has its own staff of teachers (a body of 'fellows'), who give personal instruction to the students of the college—though they also, for the most part, give public lectures in addition to the students of the university as a whole. A college may thus be defined as a unit both of residence and of education in which both teachers and students join together in a common life. The

[1] The words of Cardinal Newman are famous (in *The Idea of a University*): 'I protest to you . . . that if I had to choose between a so-called University, which dispensed with residence and tutorial super-intendence, and gave its degrees to any person who passed an examination in a wide range of subjects, and a University which had no professors or examinations at all, but merely brought a number of young men together for three or four years, and then sent them away . . . I have no hesitation in giving the preference to that University which did nothing, over that which exacted of its members an acquaintance with every science under the sun.'

colleges are almost as old as the universities themselves: their foundation began in the thirteenth century, and it continued until the beginning of the seventeenth century. There are about twenty Colleges in each of the universities: the average number of their students in Oxford is about 160, and in Cambridge about 270.

The existence of these colleges permits, and indeed requires, the two old universities to assume a federal character, with that division of functions between the central or 'federal' authority and the various 'State' or 'provincial' authorities which is characteristic of federations. It also permits, though it does not require, that larger size which is generally a characteristic of federations. The other universities, in comparison, are of the nature of 'unitary' States: each is a single and undivided body; and each, accordingly, is smaller in size. But two qualifications must at once be added to this statement. The first is that two of the other universities—the University of London and the University of Wales—are both federal. Nominally, like Oxford and Cambridge, they are federations of colleges. Actually, however, they are federations of universities; for many of their constituent colleges—University College, for example, in the University of London, and the college at Cardiff in the University of Wales—are themselves of the nature and dimensions of universities.[1] The second qualification is that in Scotland there is one unitary university, Glasgow, which, with 5,000 students, is larger than Oxford and nearly as large as Cambridge. Glasgow, however, and to a less degree Edinburgh (with 3,600 students), are both exceptional among the unitary universities of Great Britain.

[1] University College, with 1,850 students, is larger than any of the modern English universities, except Manchester, which has a little over 2,000. Similarly the college at Cardiff, with 1,000 students, is larger than three of the English universities (Bristol, Reading, and Sheffield), each of which has under 1,000 students.

We have seen that the two old universities have a residential character; we have also seen that they have a federal character. It remains to add that they have a tutorial character. This is connected with, and flows from, the existence of colleges. When there are colleges existing and acting as units of education within the general educational system of the university, it becomes possible to add to the general system of instruction by lecture, which is given in the university, a further system of individual 'tuition' or 'supervision', which is given in the college, either to the individual student or to a small group of two or three. This adds an element of personal and individual contact which is obviously of no little value. But such tuition is not only connected with the college system: it is also connected with the system of Honours courses. It is the Honours student, generally engaged in the intensive study of some single subject,[1] to whom tuition can be most profitably given, and to whom it is particularly given. Wherever, therefore, there is a system of Honours courses, individual tuition will also appear, even if there are no colleges as its basis; and in the newer universities (Manchester, London, and elsewhere) it has already appeared and is spreading. It is obvious, however, that the existence of separate staffs in colleges (in addition to the University Professoriate) greatly facilitates the working of a system of individual tuition in the old universities.

The question is sometimes asked whether the old universities are 'class' universities. It must be admitted that there are many rich men among their students. It must also be admitted that the normal cost of residence for the twenty-

---

[1] Sometimes an Honours Course (e.g. the Oxford courses in *Literae Humaniores* and in Modern Philosophy, Politics, and Economics, or the Cambridge course in Part I of the Natural Sciences Tripos) consists of a group of connected subjects; but generally in British universities an Honours Course is devoted to some one subject such as English. or History, or French, or Chemistry, or Botany.

four weeks of term at the old universities is greater (perhaps by some £60 to £90 per annum) than the cost of residence for the thirty weeks of term at the newer universities. On the other hand, as we have already seen, the number of assisted students at the old universities is practically the same as the number at the newer English universities. Nor is there any gulf between these students and the others in either of the old universities. They all live together, on equal terms, in their colleges: they all share in the same games and activities: there is no *corps d'élite*, and, on the contrary, there is a good deal of *esprit de corps*. In almost every range of student life Oxford and Cambridge are genuinely democratic communities; and even if some well-to-do butterflies survive, they are mixed with the bees, and they are being assimilated to the bees with which they are mixed. Meanwhile, it is good to remember that 'it takes all sorts to make a world'. And a university, after all, is a miniature world.

The New Universities

The work which the new universities have achieved is one of the most remarkable chapters in the history of British universities. We are here concerned not with the Scottish universities, which have a great and distinguished history of their own, but with the newer universities of England and Wales. Though their beginnings go back for nearly a hundred years, it is only during the present century, and within the last twenty-five years (since the Education Act of 1902, which first provided them with the necessary basis of a system of secondary education), that they have really been able to get seriously to work. Their progress has been astonishing. They are educating to-day some of the soundest and most typical elements of England and Wales. They are developing as quickly as they can the residential and tutorial characteristics which were once thought to be peculiar to the old universities. Though they owed their origin, in a large measure, to the mid-Victorian sense of the importance of applied science, none of them can now be justly described as specialized or technological institutions: they are all *studia generalia*, in the old medieval sense. They are all seeking to fulfil the various purposes of a university—the education of its undergraduate members, the conduct and promotion of research, the provision of extra-mural instruction. Sometimes a distinguished professor, or a group of distinguished professors, in some particular subject, has made one of the newer universities a leader for the whole country. It is invidious to particularize. But an example has value; and it is perhaps permissible to mention the Manchester school of historical research, in the days of Sir Adolphus Ward, Professor Tout, Professor Tait, and their successors.

The peculiarity, the strength, and (in a small measure) the weakness of the newer universities is their local, their 'provincial', their 'civic' character.[1] They are rooted in their own areas: they are immersed in the life of their own regions. This is a weakness, in so far as their students, during their whole career, from the primary and secondary school to the university, may continue in the same district, without coming necessarily into any contact with students from other

[1] The University of London raises peculiar considerations. We may call it 'imperial', when we reflect that 1,000 of its 'internal' students are drawn from the British Empire (as compared with 480 in Edinburgh, 360 in Cambridge, and 325 in Oxford), or when we reflect that through its system of 'external' students it is in close contact with Ceylon and other parts of the Empire. We may call it 'national', when we remember that (including medical students) nearly one-third of its total of 9,000 students is drawn from parts of Great Britain outside the London radius. But so far as the evidence of numbers goes we may perhaps most justly call it 'metropolitan' (over one-half of its students are drawn from the London area), and we may thus set it by the side of the 'civic' or 'provincial' Universities of Birmingham, Leeds, and Manchester. Yet London remains a 'mixed' university; and the future alone can decide its predominant character.

districts. But what is a weakness is also, from another point of view, a source of strength and vitality. There is local patriotism and local support behind these universities; and they, in their turn, are something of a power in local life and local problems. There is such a thing as academic anaemia; and the newer universities are preserved from that peril by being plunged into the circulation and the throb of the workaday life of a great civic community. It is a possible weakness of the old universities—national bodies set in small civic communities with a large and tolerably bare rural area stretching around them—that they should be dreaming sojourners, standing 'like Ruth amid the alien corn'. But here again what is a weakness is also a strength; and if Oxford and Cambridge, by their very position, stand somewhat apart from the busy life of the market-place, they also stand aloof from the 'idols' and standards of the market-place. Nor have they been reluctant to plunge into the great currents of national life. It was Cambridge which started the system of 'extension' lectures: it was Oxford which started the system of 'tutorial classes' among working men and women; and they are both attempting, at the present time, a scheme of rural education in the villages of their surrounding counties. This is all to the good. And moreover one has to remember that, if Goethe said that a character builds itself 'in the stream of the world', he also said that 'a talent builds itself in stillness'. Academic anaemia is dangerous; but academic 'stillness' is beatitudinous.

Defects and Dangers of British Universities

A foreign observer might perhaps criticize British universities, and particularly the older universities, for the peculiar nature of the emphasis which they lay on the building of character. The tutorial system, under which the tutor of a college is concerned not only with his student's intellectual development, but also with his behaviour: the 'proctorial' system, under which university officers of discipline (in addition to those of the colleges) are concerned with offences against manners and morals—both of these may be said to regard character, and to regard it in a self-defeating way, because instead of letting it grow they seek to control its growth. But it is difficult even for universities, though they deal with grown men, to escape from the ethical strain which runs through the educational system of Great Britain.

Some would refuse to count this strain for a merit: few would regard it as a very serious defect. If we seek to count the serious defects of British universities, we shall find them in other quarters. One, as we have already seen reason to notice, is the imperfect organization of advanced study, more particularly in the various branches of the arts. This is a grave defect; and connected with it (though it does not go far to explain it) is an imperfect provision of post-graduate or research studentships. Moreover, while students of promise are too often deprived of the chance of engaging in advanced study, professors who should be directing and conducting research are often engrossed and diverted from their essential function by the pressure of administrative duties. Another defect is a certain crowding, which has become marked in late years, of the undergraduate courses in the various branches of arts—a crowding due to the tendency of students to move towards the salaries and the safety of the teaching and similar professions. Again, it may be urged, with some justice, that the extra-mural work of the universities has its risks as well as its advantages. Its advantages are indeed great. It brings the universities, and particularly the older universities, into a closer touch with the general community; and it would be a dereliction of social conscience to drop, or curtail, such work. It is also work which is largely conducted by special teachers; and to that extent it does not add any further burden to the ordinary teachers of universities. Yet it must remain a charge on the energy and the spirit of some, at any rate, of the members of each university; and for that reason it is possible not, indeed, to urge its reduction, but at any rate to deprecate its expansion.

In a broader sense, and rising above the three particular matters which have just been mentioned, we may say that Great Britain has recently and suddenly realized the value of university education. The awakening began with the overhauling and the increase of secondary education by the Education Act of 1902, which resulted in a great extension of the field of recruitment for universities. It was hastened and accentuated by the experience of the War. The danger of a sudden awakening and a rapid conversion is that they may result in the policy of the opposite extreme. The nation may, as it were, over-value its universities: it may run away with the idea that it is impossible to have too much of a good thing. Those who know our universities best are haunted by the fear that a democratic enthusiasm, as genuine as it is ill-informed, may result in an attempt to increase the quantity of university education at the expense of its quality. On the one hand, too many students may be forced into the existing universities, with a consequent lowering of their standards: on the other hand, new universities may be created before those already in existence have been properly based and have secured an adequate measure of support. After all, the supply of first-rate minds for the filling of university staffs is not unlimited; and it is significant that a great German scholar, in his *Recollections*, has asked the question, 'Does our nation really produce so many talents as are required for the filling of the chairs at our Universities?' An English scholar might put the same question with even greater force.

The danger of a fervid democratic enthusiasm is met, and

enhanced, by the danger of technical zeal. 'The Universities', men say, 'are the homes of the finest training: why should they not train not only our doctors, dentists, and veterinary surgeons—not only our engineers, civil, mechanical, electrical, and chemical—but also our elementary teachers, our journalists, and the members of all our professions?' Or again, 'The Universities', it may be said, 'are supposed to possess the finest knowledge and the acutest skill: why should they not apply both, especially as they are so largely supported by public funds, to the improvement of our brewing, our textiles, our glass, our chemical industries?' The teachers of our universities, partly in modesty and partly in ambition, but altogether from a feeling that they must 'do something for the country', may listen too readily to such appeals. But it is a great mistake, as some of the American universities have found, to blur the distinction between the university and the technical college. It is here that Oxford and Cambridge can be of peculiar service, because they have a peculiar power, from their very position, of keeping the true and pure 'idea of a University'. The other universities are exposed to a far greater pressure: the old universities, just because they are less exposed, have a great and bounden duty of defending, for the sake of the rest, the stronghold of pure learning and long-time values against the demands of material progress and the zest for immediate values and quick returns.

The dangers of British universities are the dangers which might be expected in a country such as Great Britain. A country of practical men, with a good deal of 'handiness' and a large amount of social interest, will naturally breed universities which reflect its own qualities. Its universities will tend to be 'handy' institutions, ready to examine schools, to undertake extra-mural work, to furnish all the professions and even the world of business with recruits, to provide members for commissions and committees (alike in Church and in State)—in short to do a number of useful (nay, necessary) things, over and above the *unum necessarium* of 'the study and advancement of the higher branches of learning'. It is an old complaint of Bacon, 'Amongst so many great foundations of colleges in Europe, I find it strange that they are all dedicated to professions, and none left free to arts and sciences at large'; and it is an old and memorable warning, of the same great thinker, 'If any man think philosophy and universality to be idle studies, he doth not consider that all professions are from thence served and supplied'. Philosophy and universality remain the alpha and omega of British universities; it was in this that they began, and it will be to this that they will always necessarily return. We admit that if they have their temptation—the temptation of being also among the social prophets and servants—it is not an ignoble one; indeed it is one which modern universities share also with modern churches. But the university, like the Church, lives by the Spirit, and for the cultivation of the things of the Spirit; and like all other spiritual institutions it must always be judged, in the last resort, by the degree to which it performs its own intimate and essential purpose.

American Universities as Institutions of Learning[1]

By ABRAHAM FLEXNER

(Director of the Institute for Advanced Study, New York.)

IT is extremely difficult to write a brief account of American universities. The reason is simple. Universities have never been identical in all countries. It has, however, always been possible to discuss German, French, or Scandinavian universities in general terms. In England, that has been less easy, since Oxford and Cambridge represent one type, London another, and the Provincial universities a third. In America, the term 'university' is still more loosely used and abused. There are American 'universities' that enforce no scholastic standards whatever; others that are the playthings of politicians; others that are not merely disfigured by, but buried beneath, utterly irrelevant departments and schools; a few which approximate to institutions of learning.

For, as I view the subject, a university is primarily an institution of learning; and a modern university differs from a medieval university mainly because new activities and problems have become objects of intellectual curiosity and social importance. The moment one makes this admission, other consequences follow. If new and various objects of

[1] The two contributions on the American universities have been worked out independently and without previous consultation between the authors.

intellectual curiosity and social importance demand the attention of scholars and scientists, then other activities of lower grade must be lopped off and taken care of in some other appropriate way. The mere teaching function recedes; research, investigation, the education of promising scholars in the technique of training and research come to the front. The two functions cannot to-day be combined, as the American university with its graduate school and undergraduate college tries to combine them; for the number of students becomes unwieldy and the faculty is distracted between two inconsistent responsibilities—teaching boys and educating men.

No American institution has yet acted upon this distinction. In consequence, American universities look like bedlam. They have, to be sure, made great strides. They have amassed large endowments; they have acquired beautiful buildings; many of them possess laboratories and libraries that are not excelled anywhere in the world; in their huge faculties may be found a very considerable number of men of international repute—not only of physicists and chemists and mathematicians, but Hellenists, latinists, orientalists, medievalists, historians, economists, physicians, publicists, &c.

In my opinion the university should stop with these, leaving all other educational tasks to be otherwise provided for. No American university takes this view. All of them possess colleges, which are secondary schools, inferior in solidity to the secondary schools of England and the Continent. Many of them possess teacher training departments, in which an absurdly artificial technique is communicated to an inferior student body—this being one of several reasons for the poor quality of the American high school and elementary school; even more common are business departments, schools of journalism, schools of practical arts, and even a department of hotel management. Not satisfied with the miscellaneous aggregation thus brought together to reside in the university, correspondence and home study courses are organized, which endeavour to give by mail the equivalent of resident study. Most of this is, of course, business, not education; it is not even 'service', the catchword by which it is usually designated. Yet it flourishes in institutions like Columbia, Chicago, and the State universities, which issue false and misleading advertisements, bulletins, and circulars, like vendors of patent medicines. This is 'service'—but it is 'service' that pays! In a single year Columbia University thus earned $300,000.

I have tried briefly to indicate the good and the bad sides of American universities. But my account would not be fair if I omitted the human side. Backward as our student body is in respect of intellectual maturity, it is in general, socially, a wholesome group of fine boys and girls, who mature quickly in the actual struggles of life. They know less than their European contemporaries, though they are two years older; their cultural interests are so limited as to be merely accidental; but they are 'good fellows' and such they usually remain. Perhaps European education has overstressed the intellectual element; American education throughout overstresses the social element. In consequence, not even the graduate schools of the best of our universities contain a majority of students fit to utilize the opportunities spread before them. When will this situation change? When will the college be in whole or part detached? When will organized athletics, fraternities and extra-curricular activities in general be relegated to their proper—and subordinate—place? When will University Presidents cease to be noisy personages, and be proud to remain academic aides? When will money be diverted from bricks and mortar in order to support brains on a dignified and self-respecting basis? When will some university discard riff-raff in the shape of business, journalism, &c., in order to become a home for scholars and scientists seeking to understand a distraught world? No one knows. The American university has done well to attack realities; but it has done little in the way of holding fast to the distinction between the relevant and important, on the one hand, the irrelevant and unimportant, on the other.

Higher Education in the United States

By CLARENCE SHEDD

Introduction

The term 'university' is loosely used in America, covering not only first-rate university organizations but frequently small undergraduate colleges where its use may be regarded as a symbol of the faith of the founders. This use of the term by some Class B or C colleges is ridiculous and causes much misunderstanding at home and abroad. Frequently, however, it is used by very high grade colleges which have no university pretensions, but where for historical and sentimental reasons a change of name does not seem possible. In spite, however, of these exceptions, there has grown up in American higher education during the past fifty years a commonly accepted meaning for the idea of the university—a meaning that would be acknowledged by institutions that in their names and practices deny its fundamental validity.

In the United States the university is an association of undergraduate Colleges of Arts and Sciences, graduate and professional schools, and the research institutes, libraries, and museums essential to the tasks involved in the pursuit and advancement of learning. The colleges and schools associated in the university organization are under the general control of a university Board of Trustees (Harvard, Board of Overseers); but this control is related primarily to problems of general policy, particularly finances, endowments, buildings, ultimate decisions as to appointments and broad educational policy. The individual colleges and schools within the university have very large and, for all practical purposes, complete freedom on matters of educational policy and major influence in the determination of the teaching personnel. The members teaching in the same field of knowledge in the different schools of the university form a Department and from this departmental organization comes much of the initiative for scholarly studies and research.

As in England *the undergraduate college is the heart of the university*, but its faculty is as much involved in the obligations for research as are the faculties of the graduate and professional schools. The college is the object of the deepest affections and finest loyalties among American university people, but it is also the source of a large proportion of the problems that distress the American university as it confronts the modern world. In recent years there have been in the United States and abroad many criticisms of the American university based on a conception that ignores the central place of the undergraduate college in the university. Valuable and stimulating as are such criticisms, they lack a fair sense of proportion and because of their fundamental assumptions inevitably miss some of the most difficult of America's university problems, besides failing to take adequate account of the creative contributions of the university in the field of higher education. The conception of the university as an institution primarily devoted to the pursuit of knowledge and possessing a kind of irresponsibility with regard to the relation of that knowledge to contemporary life would be generally accepted as an important part of the university ideal, but not all of it, as it misses the fact that by its history and the necessities of national life the American university has been pre-eminently a learning and teaching institution. Even to-day no one figure colours American educational discussion more than the conception of a university as 'Mark Hopkins (the perfect teacher) on one end of a log and a student on the other'. This conception of the intimate co-operative work of student and teacher as members of a community of learning, involving mutual obligations that cannot be limited to the class-room, must be constantly at the centre if one is to have a fair judgement of higher education in the United States to-day. However far the practices of colleges and universities have led them astray from this ideal, it nevertheless remains the conception that is most universally accepted. In this picture scholarship and research are indissolubly associated with the work of teaching, but research must never be an excuse for bad teaching. There is no good teaching without sound scholarship, but in the United States, as in other countries, there is much atrocious teaching by men about whose high scholarship there can be no question.

The abstract pursuit of knowledge for its own sake or for immediate or ultimate community or national scientific purposes has never had as large a place in American universities as at the present time. An examination of the presidential and research reports of the universities will make this clear. As judged by any fair criteria American universities have fallen far short of producing their reasonable proportion of the world's great scholars and scientists. It is significant, however, that at a time when the universities are being subjected to the most violent criticisms there are more internationally known names of first rank in the fields of the physical, psychological and social sciences and in the field of educational philosophy than have appeared at any previous time in our educational history. It is less than a half-century since the last frontier was settled in the United States, and the crudities of a pioneering and geographically isolated democracy still cling to many of its social institutions, including its institutions of higher learning. There is an inevitable lack of cultural maturity for which such words as 'thinness' and 'superficiality' are not quite adequate.

Intimate as the association between research and the university must always be, nothing seems clearer at the present moment than that the scholarly research in the humanities and sciences demanded by our complex age can no longer be the exclusive prerogative of the university. This was a tenable university conception for a relatively simple social order in which the university enjoyed prestige, rights, and immunities because it (with the Church) was the sole source of truth. Those rights and privileges have never existed to any considerable degree in the United States. In Germany, where this ideal was most pure, as Dr. Doerne in his able chapter makes clear, radical changes are taking place, and the university, in spite of itself, is much more involved in the hurly-burly of contemporary life and is sharing with other research institutions and foundations tasks which formerly belonged exclusively to the university. In other countries besides Germany the academic type lacks its former power for attracting youth, who find themselves part of a passionate world that seems about to fall in on them and that demands leadership vividly aware of its contemporary problems and morally prepared to meet them.

The research tasks of our world are so complex that while society looks to the university for leading influences, yet in the United States as in other countries there are developing large national research bodies (such as the Rockefeller and Carnegie Foundations) which are devoting vast sums of money to the kind of disinterested scientific research that once was the exclusive prerogative of the university. Moreover, in the United States the older universities are finding it necessary—without lessening at all the pressure on every professor to do significant and original scholarly work in his own field— to create special institutes and professorships where research is the sole task of a professor or a staff of professors who are freed from teaching responsibility.

The American undergraduate college, which is the heart of the university, will change, in fact is now radically changing; but the possibility of dissociating it from its place at the heart of the university is much more distant to-day than it was when, in the last quarter of the nineteenth century, Johns Hopkins and Clark University together pioneered the idea of a graduate university, patterned after the German universities, wholly devoted to the tasks of scientific study and research and having no undergraduate college connexions. It is quite possibly an indication of something far deeper than the thinness and superficiality of American life that, because of the educational needs of the times, both these universities developed undergraduate colleges—thus reversing the usual order in the evolution of the university.

The problem of the American university is not helped by waving aside the college as not worthy of consideration on the ground that its work is secondary in character. More will be said about this later, but at the moment it is enough to say that while half of the curriculum of the four-year college may be termed 'secondary' in the sense that it is a completion of the general culture that precedes more intensive studies, yet this with some truth may be said about the early work in universities of other countries. Changing names does not change facts, and, so long as the college occupies the place it does in the American university, the issues of American higher education cannot be met by avoiding its problems.

History of American Higher Education[1]

American higher education has its own history and it must be judged against that history. The university as described at

[1] While many reference works have been consulted and the writer has

the beginning of this chapter has only taken definite form in the last fifty years. The roots of the American university go back into English and Continental educational and religious life. The present university, however, with all its weakness and strength is distinctly the product of the necessities of a democracy in which the races of the earth have mingled, where Church and School have followed the advancing geographical frontiers, joining together in the creation of social institutions immediately essential for the life of the people. Until the beginning of the present century this pressure of the *immediate*—accentuated by the tides of immigration and the country's geographical, cultural, and psychological isolation—has been so great that it has left its mark on all institutions and particularly on education. So great has been this pressure of the immediate that while there has been a passion for schools not excelled anywhere in the world, yet until very recent years there has been no corresponding zeal for any adequate philosophy of education or for anything like a *national* system of education. The present system of American higher education is the result of the joining together of a number of fundamental ideas, which here can be outlined only in the briefest fashion.

The whole American system of free public education is more indebted to the extreme Calvinism of the early New England colonists than to any other one single force in American life. These early colonists formed a government in which there were no lines separating Church from State. The insistence of Calvinism on the Bible as central to salvation, and the necessity of a literate laity that was a concomitant of this idea, account for the fact that as early as 1642 the Massachusetts colony passed a law making it obligatory upon town

done much original research on organization of colleges and student life 1700–1850, yet he desires to acknowledge a major dependence on *Public Education in the United States*, by E. P. Cubberly, for the general outline and many of the facts contained in this historical section.

officials to ascertain if parents and masters were training their children, so that they could 'read and understand the principles of religion and the capital laws of the country'. The child was to be educated because the necessities of religion demand it, and also because the State would suffer if he were not educated. Shortly after this the introduction of public taxation for the education of children carried the principle of State and parental responsibility one step farther.

Another contribution of Calvinism appeared most sharply in the field of higher education. Religion is indissolubly associated with the history of American higher education. When John Harvard (1638) 'dreading to leave an illiterate ministry to the Church when our ministers shall lie in their graves' made a gift of £779 for the endowment of Harvard College, Boston was then a village of only two score houses and but twenty-five towns had been settled in Massachusetts. Cotton Mather (1702) said 'the college was the best thing that ever New England thought upon'. Until the early years of the nineteenth century the provision of an educated ministry was a dominating motive in the creation of the colonial colleges— William and Mary (Virginia), Yale, Princeton, Dartmouth, Brown, Williams, Bowdoin, and Columbia (King's College). William and Mary (1693) was founded 'that the church of Virginia may be furnished with a seminary of ministers of the gospel and that the youth may be piously educated in good letters and manners and that the Christian faith may be propagated among the Western Indians to the glory of Almighty God'. Princeton was founded by the Synod of New York in 1746 that the Church might be supplied with 'learned and able preachers of the Word'. Because Church and State were so closely related on Calvinistic lines it is not surprising to find the charter of Yale, 1701, proposing that students be so educated that they 'might be fitted for public employment both in Church and Civil State'. This note of *service to the civil state* was destined ultimately to become more dominant in American higher education than any other. As late, however, as 1820 Amherst College was established 'for the education of indigent young men for the ministry and missionary work'.

The writer in his studies of early American college history and student life has brought together from the archives of many early colleges some 350 original manuscript letters written by students who were members of early student religious societies to students in other colleges. This correspondence was international as well as intercollegiate. These letters reveal the life and atmosphere of the early colleges better than any other contemporary documents. In a letter recently discovered in the archives of the Missionary Institution of Basle, Switzerland, and sent in 1825 to students of Basle by the Society of Inquiry of Andover Seminary in the United States, there is the following paragraph which vividly describes American colleges of the time.[1]

'There are in the United States 40 or 50 Colleges containing perhaps in the whole 4,000 or 5,000 students in the various stages of education. A great proportion of these colleges and with two or three exceptions all of the most flourishing are managed more or less by the pious orthodox clergy who are thus preparing to exert an immense influence on the national character. It is proper to mention that many of these institutions especially in the Southern and Western States are yet in their infancy—without funds of which they can at present avail themselves—without libraries and without properly qualified instructors. But in their infancy yet they are objects towards which much public attention is directed. Great hopes are entertained respecting them, they are continually increasing in wealth and respectability and not a few of them are endowed with public lands which at some future period will

---

[1] I am indebted to Pastor D. Alphons Koechlin of Basle for invaluable assistance in finding this letter. The student signing this letter 'for the Society' was Leonard Bacon, grandfather of the recently-deceased Professor Benjamin W. Bacon of Yale University.

become exceedingly valuable. Those Colleges which are blessed with zealously pious instructors frequently experience revivals of religion and nearly all who become pious in such circumstances devote themselves to the work of the ministry. No wonder then that this subject should call forth the earnest and constant supplications of Christians. Many of the churches in different parts of the country not long since kept a day of special fasting and prayer for a revival of religion in all the Colleges.'

The growth of the idea that education should be at public expense was slow and in the face of great difficulties. Gradually, however, this idea won its way in the colonies. First there came the support by taxation of free elementary schools, then, beginning with Boston (1821), of the free public high school; and about the same time the beginning of the tax-supported State university. Bulletin No. 35 of the U.S. Bureau of Education (1929) reports 2,200 secondary schools in the United States with 175,000 high school teachers and an enrolment of 4,500,000. This is one of the centres around which the history of American education might well be written. It has been a story of the gradual pushing up of the level of education of the people at public expense, a movement that we shall see has not yet ceased.

It has been well said that in America there has been a devotion, one might almost say an insane passion, for schools but an inadequate concern for a national school system. Public education is a responsibility of the several States. The Federal Constitution of 1787 says nothing about education. This is understandable because in most of the colonies education was still a private responsibility. The tenth amendment to the Constitution, passed 1791, provided that all rights and duties not specifically designated as belonging to the National Government were responsibilities of the separate States. Around these two principles one can envisage the picture of the terrific difficulties involved in creating a federal union out of a group of colonies extremely jealous of one another, having quite different racial and religious backgrounds, erecting tariff walls against each other and only brought together in federal union because their essential freedom as States seemed thus to be safeguarded. Against this background it is easier to understand Washington's oft repeated but never heeded appeal for a national university 'where the youth from all parts of the United States might receive the polish of erudition in arts, sciences, and belles-lettres and where, during the juvenal period of life, when friendships are formed and habits established that stick by one, the youth or young men from different parts of the United States would be assembled together and would by degrees discover that there was not the cause for those jealousies and prejudices which one part of the union had imbibed'.

The right of individual religious denominations to have their own parochial schools and universities was a consequence both of State responsibility in education and of the right of religious liberty guaranteed by the Federal Constitution. The middle colonies represented a diverse group of religious denominations, and from the beginning did not share the views of Calvinistic New England regarding free public education or the responsibility of the State in this field. The consequence was that—with the notable exception of Benjamin Franklin's Academy (University of Pennsylvania)—the development of schools and colleges in these colonies was almost wholly under denominational influences. The movement for denominational colleges was greatly accelerated by the decision of the Supreme Court in 1819 in the Dartmouth College case. The State of New Hampshire in 1816 had attempted to make a State University out of Dartmouth College, but the ruling of the Supreme Court was that the rights and endowments of a private college were inviolate, and hence the State's action was illegal.

Something of the contemporary intensity of feeling around this issue may be seen in the following entry of March 8th, 1819, in the records of the student religious society of Dartmouth College.[1]

'The Society convened in the society Hall after being debarred from access to it one year by the would-be University. But thanks to God, The College is re-established in the possession of its former rights and privileges. We believe it to be by the kind interposition of Providence that Dartmouth College has withstood the flood of evil-doers that have risen against it. We pray the Lord to continue his kindness to the institution and its societies.— M. Chase, Sec.'

The consequence of this decision was that between 1820 and 1870 denominational colleges multiplied rapidly. As the frontiers moved westward the various church groups followed their colonists with not only churches and schools but also colleges. Until 1870 (only sixty-two years ago) the Church was the major controlling influence in American higher education. Beginning with the early years of the nineteenth century, the rapid extension of 'manhood suffrage' based on Jeffersonian conceptions of democracy, began to have a powerful influence on the development of public education, having consequences in the theory and control of primary, secondary, and higher education which brought on a half-century of bitter struggle between Church controlled and public controlled forces. The growth of public control in the primary and secondary levels of education was much more rapid than in the field of higher education and in the end the divorce between Church and State was much more complete in the elementary and secondary schools than in the colleges and universities.

Up to 1815 only four States granted the suffrage on any basis excepting that of property qualifications. By 1830 all

[1] Manuscript records, Historical Archives, Dartmouth College.

States had abolished property qualifications and created manhood suffrage. The writings of Jefferson, Madison, and Daniel Webster are full of the demand for the rapid extension of free public education from the elementary school to the university, because a democracy, granting suffrage on a manhood basis, could not be safe unless its electorate had a maximum of educational opportunity. As a token of his faith Thomas Jefferson (1819) was responsible for the magnificent beginnings of the University of Virginia; one of the finest early university creations in American educational life, freed from control by any religious denomination, owning the highest standards of scholarship and yet being fundamentally an institution of the State.

In a *Manual of American Colleges* published in 1856,[1] there are listed 154 colleges, enrolling 18,759 students. Only 14 of these are State-controlled institutions. These 14 State institutions had a total enrolment of 2,508 students, about the size of the average small State university to-day. Five thousand five hundred and eighty-one students in American colleges counted themselves as 'professors of religion'. Of this number 1,927 were preparing for the Christian ministry. It is interesting to note that the smallest percentage of 'professors of religion' was to be found in the State institutions. Only 335 of the 2,508 students were willing to classify themselves in this way. It was probably such facts as these that led to these institutions gaining a reputation for being 'Godless'. The largest enrolment in any American college at that time was Harvard, which claimed a student body of 700. Yale College came next with 605. Colleges like Bowdoin, Williams, Amherst, Princeton, Miami (Ohio), Brown, all had enrolments of between 225 and 250. Columbia College (then over 100 years old) had an enrolment of only 143 students. In the case of some present-day smaller colleges, their enrol-

[1] Z. Freeman, *Manual of American Colleges and Seminaries* (1856).

ment at that time was as large or larger than it is now. Among the State universities the largest enrolment was at the University of Virginia, where there were 514 students, 184 of whom were classified as professional students. The next largest was the University of Michigan, 288, 133 of these being medical students. The other State universities had an enrolment of 200 or less. The University of Wisconsin (then eight years old) enrolled 92 students, 30 of whom were classified as undergraduates.

In spite of constitutional limitations the National Government early recognized a responsibility for giving encouragement to higher education. Gifts of public lands as endowments for public schools and universities were the form of this help. In 1787 Congress granted two townships to the new State of Ohio for the purposes of a university. As new States were created on the frontiers similar grants of land were made for the endowment of State-controlled higher education. The most significant single act was the Morrell Land Grant Act of 1862, which gave substantial land grants and later money grants to States organizing State institutions of agriculture and mechanical arts. At about the same time the National Government created a Bureau of Education as a section of its Department of the Interior. The influence of this Bureau has steadily grown, until to-day there are strong moves in American educational circles to go a step farther and create a Secretaryship of Education in the National Cabinet.

The beginnings of the Graduate School (Yale, 1847) as an upward thrust of undergraduate departments, the gradual development of professional schools separate from the undergraduate college, and particularly the opening of Johns Hopkins and Clark University, modelled after the German university, complete the picture of the growth of the university organization. Only two general statements need to be added: one concerning the increasing influence of women in American higher education. Starting with Mount Holyoke (1837) a number of separate women's colleges developed. From this beginning have come the great group of independent women's colleges that are making such significant contributions to higher education. Beginning with Oberlin, Antioch, and the University of Iowa there came co-education, until to-day the overwhelming majority of American college students are studying in institutions where there are both men and women. The other statement concerns the influence on the American college of the elective system, introduced by President Eliot of Harvard in the 'eighties. At a time when the curriculum was relatively simple, this principle of free election brought new life and reality to American higher education. To-day in face of the multiplication and diversification of courses that has taken place, the blessings of the elective system are not so clear.

Extent and Characteristics of the Present Organization of Higher Education

The result of this historical development is that in America there are now three types of college and university control:

(1) Institutions which are wholly controlled by the State and municipalities, such as State Universities, State Colleges of Agriculture and Mechanical Arts, Normal Schools and so forth. There are 154 public-controlled institutions of higher education, more than 100 of these being State colleges and universities. Sixty-nine of the State colleges and universities are 'land grant institutions'. The results of a most comprehensive survey of these institutions have recently been published by the United States Bureau of Education. There is extremely great divergence in educational standards in this group, many being so sharply vocational as to endanger the educational standards of the colleges of liberal arts and sciences and the graduate and professional educational school

associated with these universities. Perhaps the nearest parallel to the State universities outside of the United States is to be found in 'the modern universities' of England.

(2) There are three times as many colleges more or less controlled by national Church bodies as there are State colleges and universities. Many of these Church colleges are meagrely equipped and wholly inadequate for present educational needs. In fully half of them superior educational work is being carried on. These colleges form the heart of the Association of American Colleges, which by its conferences and publications[1] is doing much for the re-creation of the liberal arts college.

(3) There are the colleges and universities that are independent either of State or Church control. In this list are most of the colonial colleges and universities which in their early foundation were institutions of the Church. The evolution from Church to private institutions is suggestive of what is taking place in American higher education in many of the Church institutions of highest worth. Many of the colleges and universities in this group are national, and to a large degree international, institutions. This would be true of all the older women's colleges—of which Mount Holyoke, Wellesley, Smith, Vassar, Bryn Mawr are examples. Harvard, Yale, Princeton, Dartmouth, Columbia, Massachusetts Institute of Technology, and the University of Chicago, among the larger institutions, and Williams, Amherst, Swarthmore among the smaller colleges, are some of the institutions in this group that draw their students from the nation at large.

Between 800 and 900 colleges, universities, and professional schools report to the United States Bureau of Education. They involve an enrolment of fully 900,000

[1] The most recent and most valuable publication is *The Effective College*, edited by Robert Lincoln Kelly, secretary of this Association.

full-time college and university students. Partial statistics for the college year 1931–2, published in the December 12th, 1931, issue of *School and Society* by Dean Raymond Walters of Swarthmore College, show that 444 of these colleges report this year an enrolment of more than 560,000 full-time students, an enrolment that has not decreased from last year in spite of the economic depression. For the last two or three years the small percentage of increase has been in marked contrast to the great increases of the earlier after-War years. It should, however, be noted that an enrolment which maintains the rate of increase that had been attained by 1930 still creates those problems associated with overcrowding which are troubling educators in all countries, and particularly in the United States and Germany.

There are more than 10,000 students from foreign countries enrolled in the universities of the United States. They come from 111 countries, Canada, China, Japan, the Philippines, Russia, England, and Germany leading. The marked increase in the number of students coming from Germany is of significance, and in sharp contrast to the early years of the twentieth century, when few German students came to the United States. Nearly half of the foreign students are scattered across the country, enrolled in smaller colleges and universities. The majority, however, are concentrated in the big university centres—both private and State controlled. In big university centres like New York, Chicago, and Berkeley (California), the generosity of Mr. John D. Rockefeller, Junior, has made possible the erection of great international houses as centres for hospitality and international life for these 'guest students'. An extensive national programme of friendly service for guest students is carried on under the leadership of the Institute of International Education and the National Committee for Friendly Relations with Foreign

Students, which works in co-operation with the universities and with the leaders of the Churches and Student Christian Movement.

While in 1931–2 the number of women students in the colleges is fewer than in the previous year—undoubtedly because of economic conditions—yet the figures of 1931, when compared with those of ten years ago, show that the percentage of gain in the enrolment of women students is proportionately greater than in the enrolment for men students.

Comparative statistics also make dramatically clear that one of the most disturbing problems in American higher education is the rapid rise and growth of big universities in the last two decades. The major problem is, *how far can this growth go, and educational efficiency remain?* Thirty of the 444 colleges included in the statistics presented by Dean Walters contain 45 per cent. of the total university enrolment for these 444 colleges and universities. As late as 1880 there were no universities in the United States enrolling as many as 1,000 students. To-day there are more than 60 institutions with an enrolment above 2,000, and the highest ten on this list have an enrolment of full-time resident students (not including correspondence or summer session) of above 8,000. The three largest are the University of California 18,342, Columbia 15,101, and Minnesota 12,539. Since 1870 university population has increased fourteen times, whereas the general population has only a little more than trebled. In 1870 the ratio of university and college to the 1,000 of population was 1·3, whereas in 1928 it was 5·8.[1]

There are many kinds of colleges and universities. There are several hundred separate colleges of arts and sciences, some men's, some women's, and others co-educational colleges. Many technological institutions like the California

---

[1] For comparative tables see Lindsay and Holland, *College and University Administration*, p. 565.

Institute of Technology, the Massachusetts Institute of Technology, and Worcester Polytechnic Institute are quite separate from any university connexion. There are big municipal universities like the University of Cincinnati and the College of the City of New York. There are many professional schools which are independent of any university organization, schools of theology, law, medicine, dentistry, music, and commerce. There are State universities involving all of the regular schools included in the older independent universities, and also including the colleges of agriculture and mechanical arts. In some cases States have developed two separate institutions: one a general State university, and the other the State Agricultural College or College of Agriculture and Mechanical Arts.

The first degree in an American university is the Bachelor of Arts, or Bachelor of Science, representing four years of work (defined for standard Colleges of Arts and Sciences by Associations of Colleges and Universities) after the completion of four years of acceptable work in an accredited public high school or private preparatory school. The Master of Arts degree in most universities involves one year of resident work and a Master's Essay beyond the Bachelor's degree. In the case of a few of the older universities, such as Harvard and Yale, two years are required for the Master's resident and thesis work. The Ph.D. generally involves three years of extensive study beyond the A.B., the passing of comprehensive examinations in one's field, specialization and the presentation of a dissertation representing an original contribution to knowledge.

The highly organized extra-curricular life brings to the forefront an aspect of American university life with greatly mixed values. The Fraternity system with residential houses, over-occupation with many activities, athletics, particularly football, supported by alumni and the public sporting press, millions of dollars invested in immense stadia—these are all a part of a picture that gives educational leaders great concern. In the University of Minnesota, where there are more than 12,000 full-time students, a recent study showed that there were 350 different organized student groups in the university. At Northwestern during the last two or three years there has been a university-wide congress of students representing different student organizations, bringing together representatives of 150 associations of students having officers and activities. On the other hand there are many creative and educationally valid undergraduate organizations, such as debating, journalistic, literary societies, international or cosmopolitan clubs, Church student societies, Christian associations and other religious societies.

The evolution of the American university, and particularly of the big university, has forced upon college authorities the assumption of functions that have not been associated with the university until very recent years. The problem of the work-student has always been with the American university, but the development of an official university bureau to aid in finding part-time employment for such students is relatively recent. Until very recent years this has been (and still is in smaller colleges) part of the function of the college Christian associations. It is a striking fact that even in universities like Harvard, Yale, and Princeton, which draw their students from the more financially and culturally privileged groups in society, about half of the student body devote time to earning money for their education. Another function that has been thrust upon the big university is that related to physical and mental health. As an outgrowth of student initiative in competitive athletics, there have grown up physical education departments with their gymnasia, swimming pools, and valuable resources for physical health, including regular medical and psychiatric examinations.

Major Questions and Centres of Experimentation

In no time since the decade of the 'eighties have there been such fierce criticisms and so many original experiments as have characterized the past decade. A great new literature has grown up in the last ten years around American university problems. The writer has classified nearly three hundred magazine articles covering a recent three-year period and dealing with these problems. It is a time of great uncertainty and confusion, and yet in the midst of it all some of the finest educational work is being done. Any one intimately acquainted with undergraduates of even a decade ago and to-day cannot fail to realize that in the upper quarter of the better colleges and universities in the United States there are many more students of fine culture and mature intellectual interests than ever before in American college life. When comparisons are made with the more carefully selected group of European students, and those in the upper quarter of American colleges to-day, the differences in the range of culture and of ability to think independently are negligible.

There is much discussion of the aims of higher education and there are many suggestive experiments. One of the most valuable has been the Experimental College sponsored by the University of Wisconsin and led by one of America's foremost teachers, Professor Alexander Meiklejohn. In addition to its radical departures in educational method, its work was based on the assumption that there is a 'liberal understanding' which is essential even for the 'average student' and which should be thoroughly obtained before a student enters on the cultural, scientific or professional specialization of the Senior College. It also assumed that the cultures of the past could be approached as 'wholes' and not studied in segments through many separate courses, and that such study of other cultures would be significant for the social problems of our day. The recent radical changes in the curriculum of the University of Wisconsin are the best evidence of the degree of success attained by this experiment. The plan of Antioch College involves a longer period of undergraduate college work and alternating six-weeks' periods of carefully integrated academic studies and practical industrial or professional work. It is a significant challenge to fundamental and traditional conceptions of culture, as well as generally accepted ideas of educational method.

The problem of the aims of higher education has been greatly complicated since 1900 by the excessive departmentalization of knowledge and the multiplication of courses and sub-courses, until it has in many instances become almost impossible for the student to find an organizing principle for building a sound educational programme. The plan on which the undergraduate college of the University of Chicago began its work in 1931 has for one of its aims the breaking down of this excessive departmentalization of knowledge, the separation between departments and the entire lock-step requirements associated with time, credit, and grade prescriptions. The first division is the Junior College, which has its own separate faculty budget and dean, and completes the general education of the student—preparing as rapidly as possible for the more specialized work of the Senior College. The work of instruction for the Senior College is carried on under four major divisions, with faculties carrying both undergraduate and graduate work:

(*a*) The Humanities.
(*b*) The Social Sciences.
(*c*) The Physical Sciences.
(*d*) The Biological Sciences.

Within these four major divisions students will work quite independently, having the aid of general course seminars and the personal guidance of the faculty, but free to go forward as rapidly as their ability permits. Progress towards the various university degrees will be tested, not by the passing of separate courses or the accumulating of credits, but by passing comprehensive examinations administered by a Board of Examiners freed from the work of instruction. In its revolt against the traditional course examination system and the bookkeeping methods of adding up time and grade credits, it is typical of most of the new ventures in American higher education. 'It is interesting to note', says President Lowell of Harvard—himself one of the most vigorous pioneers in this field—'the progress recently made in this country by the idea of substituting for a degree based wholly on credits or courses a degree obtained by personal study in a closer field under individual guidance and tested by general examination.'

More central even than the discussion of aims are the many puzzling questions related to the unity of the four-year college. This is one of the points at which the American college is changing most rapidly. Within the past decade there has grown up a clear consensus of opinion that the unity of the American four-year undergraduate college has no longer the reality that it once possessed. The first two years of the undergraduate college curriculum is largely secondary in character and represents the completion of the work of general culture begun in the senior high school or the two upper forms of the private preparatory school. This conviction is expressing itself in many different ways; possibly one of the most dramatic has been the rapid growth of the Junior College, both public and private. The public Junior College, dealing with the first two years of undergraduate college life, has become so extensive in California that from this year Leland Stanford University largely abandons its first two undergraduate years, placing major emphasis on the Senior

College and the Graduate School. Johns Hopkins University has adopted a similar course.

There are three types of Junior Colleges.[1] There is the *public* Junior College, which is a part of the local public school system, generally an extension of the public high school. There were 46 of these in 1922 and 105 in 1927, representing an increase of 128 per cent. There is the *state* Junior College—a diverse group under State control. In 1922 there were 24 of these, and in 1927 there were 31, an increase of 29 per cent. The third group is the *private* Junior College—'private venture' or denominational schools—and of these there were 131 in 1922 and 189 in 1927, an increase of 44 per cent.

Combining the three types, the number of junior colleges in the United States has increased from 207 in 1922 to 325 in 1927, a growth of 57 per cent. The student enrolment has grown from 16,121 to 35,630, an increase of 121 per cent. The largest enrolment increase in this period, 207 per cent., was that of the public controlled group. So rapid has been the growth of the Junior College that figures for the year 1931 would undoubtedly bring the enrolments up to at least 60,000 students. The property value of Junior Colleges in 1930 was $91,000,000.

In recent years quite a few struggling denominational colleges inadequately equipped for four-year college work have become Junior Colleges—choosing to concentrate their resources on the first two college years. There are some Junior Colleges in all States excepting Nevada, Rhode Island, Vermont, and Wyoming, but they are most prevalent in the Southern, Mid-Western, and Pacific Coast States.

With the public Junior Colleges there seem to be three

---

[1] The facts which follow on the Junior College are largely based on the writings of Leonard V. Koosand, particularly 'The Junior College', Chapter I in Kent, *Higher Education in America* (1930).

quite different functions emerging and, in true American fashion, some of these institutions are making the doubtful attempt of trying to combine all three. The first is that of providing the equivalent of the first two years' work of a Grade A college. Where this can be done well, it makes it possible for a student to continue his studies in his home community for two years beyond the high school period, greatly reducing the cost of college education for the student. It also relieves the overcrowded universities for those two years and frees the university for its more advanced work. A second function is that of rounding off the general cultural training of the high school for those who will not go on to the university. From the standpoint of the university this should tend to eliminate many who are never able to go beyond the first two years of university work. It is quite probable that in many communities the last two high school years will be joined with the Junior College, making a 'people's college' and giving a unity to secondary education that it does not now have. There can be little doubt that the spread of this movement tends to push the level of free public education up two years higher—it is another upward thrust in the movement for the general education of the nation's future citizens. A third function is that of providing adequate vocational training for those whose educational needs are not now adequately met by the public high schools, and cannot possibly be met by the cultural, scientific, or professional curricula of the university.

It is not yet clear exactly how this development will affect either the separate four-year college or the college in the university. Other large universities may follow the example of Leland Stanford and Johns Hopkins and welcome it as freeing them from secondary teaching and enabling them to devote their energies more exclusively to graduate and professional school work. This development seems quite unlikely, because with the older universities there is an unwillingness to believe that the general cultural work of the first two years is wholly secondary in character, or that it can be separated from the more intensive cultural specialization of the Senior College without loss to both and to later graduate and professional studies. The pressure of the Junior College on the separate four-year college will be such as to force the better colleges to do their first two years of work in a superior way and to force inadequately equipped colleges either to concentrate on the first two years, cease to exist, or combine with other struggling small colleges.

In many quarters there is a strong conviction that much of the general cultural work now done in the first two college years might be largely done in the senior high school, and by intensive work be completed in the first year of the undergraduate college, thereby saving one year. This has been one aspect of the common Freshman year plan of Yale College. Whether or not the work begun in the secondary school for the development of a general liberal culture can be completed in less time than the first two years of college, there is growing unanimity of opinion regarding the two upper years of college. These are years of concentration and will be more intimately connected with the Graduate School than formerly. At Harvard, Princeton, Yale, Smith, and many other colleges this move has expressed itself by the introduction of much more freedom in the last two undergraduate years and much more intensive cultural or scientific specialization. This does not mean specialization from the standpoint of pre-professional courses, although in many universities this is already an option for the student. Generally, however, it means specialization in a fundamental field of knowledge, such as the social sciences or physical sciences, leading towards more intensive work in the Graduate School.

Closely associated with this remaking of the four-year

college are a whole series of questions and problems forced on American universities by the overcrowding since the close of the World War. These great numbers of students have put an unbearable strain on the educational and financial resources of many universities. During the last decade an extensive literature has grown up around the problem of who should go to college, with some educators favouring the sharp limitation of collegiate and graduate education to a small 'intellectual aristocracy'. An important by-product of this issue is the question of the selection and admission of students. In the independent colleges and many of the church colleges in the last few years there has been a constant raising of standards of admission. Competition for numbers has ceased and a contest for qualitative excellence has begun. This problem of methods of selection and admission of students is obviously a more difficult one for the free State universities, attended as they are by nearly half of the students of university grade in the country. In most cases they are required by law to accept any students who have creditably finished the course in the public high schools of the State. Gradually, however, certain factors are changing this situation; the sense of the social cost as well as the individual tragedy of bad selection is dawning upon educators.

Many studies of the causes of failure in college show that from 25 per cent. to 50 per cent. of those entering either lack the qualifications for college work or have been inadequately prepared. With a more adequate programme of educational guidance these students would have been directed to vocational training schools, where they would have done excellent work and been saved from the psychology of failure. The University of Minnesota studies revealed that 30 per cent. were unable to continue college after the Freshman year, and 20 per cent. more were obliged to leave at the end of the Sophomore year. Between 30 per cent. and 40 per cent.

lacked the qualifications for university work. Minnesota is one of the State universities that is courageously dealing with this problem and its situation may be taken as typical of that confronting many of the public-controlled universities.[1] This overcrowding, however, has worked to the advantage of private-controlled colleges and universities, because the pressure of large numbers demanding entrance into the universities has enabled them to raise substantially their admission requirements, and much more carefully select their students than formerly. The raising of the standards by these colleges tends, in turn, to raise standards in public institutions. This has been true not only of the larger independent universities, but of scores of smaller colleges. Middlebury College (Vermont), one of the smaller and older coeducational liberal arts colleges, has in the past few years in spite of raised standards been able to select its entering class from a list of applicants that was from two to four times greater than the number that could be admitted.

The ordinary methods of selection in American colleges have been three:

(1) Examinations set by the individual college. This method has almost if not wholly disappeared in favour of the second.

(2) Examinations set by an intercollegiate examining board—the College Entrance Examination Board organized in 1900 and functioning largely for the eastern colleges and universities. In 1926 this board conducted the examinations of 22,089 candidates of 1,869 schools (1,040 public high schools and 829 private schools), at 321 examination centres.[2] The majority of these students were candidates for admission

---

[1] One of the most adequate symposia on present problems and experiments in American higher education is *Problems of College Education* (Paul Hudson, Editor), University of Minnesota Press (1928).

[2] David Allan Robertson, *American Colleges and Universities*, p. 20.

to New England and Middle Atlantic States colleges. This Board has been the most significant single factor in the establishment and raising of college entrance standards and its work powerfully influences the teaching of the public high schools and private preparatory schools. For a school to have a large proportion of its graduates fail to pass the Board's examinations is a reflection of a most serious nature on the curriculum and teaching of the school.

This admission plan has not, however, been without its evils. With the growth of the Board's power there came also the development of professional tutoring schools in which students who had failed on the basis of their secondary school training were by a 'cramming' process enabled to pass these examinations. Space does not permit the detailing of the Board's new plan of examinations, but suffice it to say that it largely does away with these evils.

(3) The certificate plan is the basis for admission of the overwhelming majority of university students. The assumption underlying this plan is, that in the long run the student's qualification for admission is better tested by the frequent examinations of his secondary school teachers than by any examinations set up by the colleges themselves, with the proviso, of course, that the colleges themselves have some control of the content of curriculum and quality of instruction in the schools. Around this idea there have grown up regional associations of schools and colleges which have as a part of their functions the developing of standards and building up of lists of accredited schools. This plan too has many dangers associated with it, not the least of which comes from the difficulty of maintaining any uniformity of high standards with hundreds of inadequately manned secondary schools, where teachers and principals change with alarming frequency. It is an even more acute problem with the hundreds of small town one- and two-teacher high schools. This has

become much more serious with the overworked condition both of schools and colleges in the last decade.

These problems have forced the colleges to seek other ways of testing the qualifications of applicants. Many are now developing—particularly with the older independent colleges which are freer to pioneer than the State institutions. There is very wide use of various psychological tests for intelligence, scholastic aptitude, and social attitudes. These tests are being used, not as substitutes for certificates or examinations, but as supplementary evidence. The developing experience in the construction and use of these tests shows that they have an extremely high reliability as a basis for prediction of scholarly interests and achievement. Even in the larger universities heroic efforts are being made to re-establish the personal relationships between college and applicant that existed a generation ago when all colleges were small, and the personal interview with the dean or president was regarded as the most important factor in the admission of a candidate. The personnel bureaux in large universities are making substantial contributions at this point. The records of interests and scholastic achievement are much more elaborate and give to the college a much more graphic picture of the student's possibilities. Even more significant than these is a growing tendency on the part of many of the universities with highest standards to consider only students whose academic work places them in the upper quarter or upper third in scholastic ability of the graduating class of any school.

The problem of the student of superior ability in the big university, where class-room work and the whole organization of the university tend to be 'levelled down' to meet the needs of the average student, has been another important factor in the discussions of overcrowding and the selection of students. There are no prospects of any reversal of the fundamentally American policy of offering the maximum educational opportunity to each individual, in favour of limiting higher education to an intellectual aristocracy. This has not resolved itself into an 'either-or debate', where the choice must be made between the needs of the average student and the student of superior ability. The needs of both must be met.

Out of all these discussions is coming a great new series of experiments dealing with the student of superior ability—experiments that are beginning to have their effect also on the problem of the average student. Swarthmore College, beginning 1922, pioneered in the development of honour courses for students, beginning with the Junior year, a plan borrowed from the English universities and involving a much higher degree of freedom from attendance at classes or lectures and independent study under the guidance of a tutor —the work to be of very high grade. Of the bigger universities Princeton, with a highly developed tutorial system, and Harvard, with a tutorial system, comprehensive examinations, and periods in the university year free for reading, have done much to forward this pioneering. The honours course plan has spread rapidly in American universities and to-day is found in some form in nearly 200 institutions—including many State universities.

Another related plan has been that of sectioning large classes on the basis of ability—thus making it possible for students in a large university to pursue their studies in immediate comradeship with students of their own level of intellectual ability. Perhaps one of the consequences of centring attention on the student of superior ability has been the strengthening of the conviction that educational methods valuable for the honours group may with some adaptations point the way to more creative methods of instruction for students of average ability. There are, of course, seemingly insuperable obstacles in the way of costs, but they are certainly no greater than those met at other stages in the history of American higher education.

Another disturbing problem is the question of the big university. Can universities grow beyond a certain size and be effective educationally? When is a university so large that the possibilities of doing creative scholarly work cease? Harvard and Yale are taking the lead here by giving one answer to this question. Because of the generosity to both universities of Mr. Edward Harkness, they are now beginning to break down their large colleges of liberal arts and group them into small residential units containing 200 to 300 students each, and capable of strong scholarly interest and achievement in close association with instructors and tutors. While at present the 'house plan' is not the exact equivalent of the relation of the colleges of Oxford and Cambridge to the university, yet it is to them that the plan obviously owes its inspiration. The important fact is that these experiments vividly suggest the conviction that the best educational work can only be done where the community is small enough to make possible vital comradeship between students and faculty in the co-operative tasks involved in learning and teaching.

Because of the very great expense involved in these plans, it is not probable that many large universities will be able to follow this lead by Harvard and Yale. The experiments will, however, throw light, of wide significance, on a number of the most serious difficulties plaguing American universities at the present moment. That other universities will find different ways of restoring that intimacy of relationship and sense of partnership in the scholarly tasks of a university community that is so central to the best work, there can be little doubt.

These and similar experiments put a new light on the problem of the place of the small college in American higher education. Within the past decade many have been saying that the small college must go. The dawning sense of the superficial work that is almost inevitably associated with bigness does not make the answer to the problem of the small college quite as clear as 'it seemed in the past. There is no doubt that many of the small colleges in the United States should disappear, not because they are small but because there is no reasonable hope of their having the resources for being serious and adequate educational institutions for days like the present. If the small colleges will cease their attempts to duplicate the widely diversified curriculum of the big universities and, like Swarthmore, Whittier, Rollins, and Reed, and many other small colleges, choose educational excellence as their main reason for existence, then it is possible that the most significant contributions to higher education in the next two decades may come from this source.

There is no room for adequate discussion of the relation of extra-curricular activities to the curriculum.[1] Perhaps it is enough to say that there are forward-looking experiments pointing towards a time when the so-called extra-curricular activities will be so related to different aspects of the curriculum as to be the informal educational processes of the university community, finding much of their stimulus from the class-room itself. Only a word can be said about football. The early action of a Committee of the Association of American University Professors has helped a great deal. The recent report of the Carnegie Foundation's investigation of American football is perhaps the most useful contribution to this problem that has been made for years. This exposure of the evils of professionalism—excessive salaries for football coaches, the power of the sporting press—has stirred under-

---

[1] Among many recent special studies in this field two deserve special mention: (a) H. Stuart Chapin, *Extra-curricular Activities at the University of Minnesota*, University of Minnesota Press (1929), and (b) A. B. Crawford, *Incentives to Study*, Yale University Press (1929).

graduates as well as faculty, as no other discussion of this problem has done for many years. At the present moment the picture of the forty-five deaths resulting from inter-collegiate football in the fall of 1931, and the tragic death of the West Point player at the Yale-Army game, has had a sobering effect on the American public. The most significant thing, however, in the football situation is that in the older colleges, which in the beginning were responsible for the place taken by football in college life, there has been a steadily growing indifference to football on the part of college undergraduates. People not intimately acquainted with student life do not know that at Harvard and Yale for the last four or five years it has been impossible to get students to attend the rallies for the team that in other days were a final test of loyalty to the college. In a number of institutions these rallies, with all they symbolize, have been done away with. Student objection in one large university to the over-emphasis on football forced the resignation of the coach. While football is still in a dramatic way in the centre of the stage so far as undergraduate activities are concerned, yet the united action of certain facultie. and of some influential groups of students is so sound and so forceful that it will in the not distant future control the relation of athletics to American higher education. It is therefore significant that along with a growing indifference on the part of undergraduates in some colleges, there has come a belated but steadily growing movement on the part of the faculty themselves to handle the problem. Ohio State and a number of other Middle Western universities have for some years had faculty control of athletics. The new plan for university direction of athletic policies at Yale is along the same line.

Perhaps at no other point has there been such great and significant progress as in the growth of co-operation and real comradeship between students and faculty in all of the curricular, extra-curricular, and student government concerns that make up the life of the modern university communities. Until the last few years student government, with its frequent dependence on 'honour systems', was in most American universities too often a device for transferring to student shoulders responsibility for many of the policing and disciplinary functions formerly carried exclusively by the faculty. The evolution to-day is towards a new form of *student and faculty* government, involving all of the concerns, formal and informal, of the life of the university community. A National Student-Faculty Conference in Detroit, Michigan, 27th–31st December, 1930, sponsored by the National University Council of Christian Associations, brought together more than 800 students and professors (about evenly divided) for the discussion of many of these common problems and their relation to religion.[1]

The inclusion of curricular problems as matters for student as well as faculty study was greatly facilitated by an event in 1923, which has proved to be of capital importance for American higher education. The chairman of the curriculum committee of Dartmouth College resigned, because he said Dartmouth students were 'doing no work, graduating without knowing anything, graduating without even wanting to know anything. The responsibility was not theirs,' he said, 'nor could it be honestly attributed to disproportionate interest in athletics.'

Out of the discussion that followed this resignation came the radical proposal that a year should be devoted to the study of the problems of education at Dartmouth, one study to be made by a selected committee of senior students (who were to receive academic credit for this work) and the other to be made by a Committee of the Faculty. The Faculty Report appeared in 1924 under the title *Study of the Liberal College*,

---

[1] For addresses at this Conference and reports of group discussions see *Education Adequate for Modern Times*, Association Press (1931).

by Professor Leon B. Richardson. In this report were sum-
marized extensive studies of work in the United States and
abroad, and it is to-day one of the most useful comparative
studies in print. The Student Report appeared shortly after
and was described as 'astonishing, brilliant and sound'. Both
reports came very close together in the radical recommendations that they made for curriculum reorganization and for
changes in the teaching procedure. As a result of these two
reports Dartmouth began on a new educational programme
which 'scrapped more than one-half of its academic procedure'. Radical as were its curriculum changes, its changes
in teaching method and in faculty-student relation were even
more far-reaching in their consequences. The substitution
of conference and tutorial methods—the elimination of course
examinations and the putting in their place of comprehensive
examinations, and the whole conception of the contribution
that students could make on curriculum organization and
teaching method, fanned into a flame the current discussions
on these problems. In many colleges and professional schools
since then radical improvements in curriculum, teaching
methods, and faculty-student relationships have come as the
result of the student-faculty studies and discussions started
by the Dartmouth College experiment. It is probably fair to
say that some of the most creative contributions being made
to international higher education now will be found in these
areas of more creative student-faculty relationships and university teaching methods.

Space has not permitted any detailed description of the
many inspiring experiments taking place in the older universities, in State universities like Michigan, Wisconsin, Minnesota, and California, or in two score of smaller colleges like
Scripps, Reed, Whittier, Swarthmore, Rollins, and Antioch,
nor in the women's colleges, such as Smith, Mount Holyoke,
Bryn Mawr, and Wellesley. In the experimental aspects of

the work of these and scores of other colleges one will find many creative changes at the point of teaching method, an enriching of the general culture of the first two years, wider opportunity for independent work and freedom from regimentation in at least the Junior and Senior years, orientation courses and other plans for breaking down the departmentalization of knowledge, new types of general and comprehensive examinations, a better integration of instruction with contemporary life and a sharp challenge to the American university tradition of degrees based on the computation of units, credits, and grades.

The limitations of this article have made impossible any discussion of equally significant changes in many graduate schools and professional schools for law, theology, and medicine. A national study of theological education, which has been in progress for two years, is bringing about radical changes in theological curriculum and method. No discussion of American universities is complete without reference to the growing concern on the part of university presidents —State and independent—for discovering better ways of effectively relating the resources of religion to the work of higher education. The encouragement given to the university pastor movement of the churches, the growing influence of the Student Christian Movement (Y.M.C.A. and Y.W.C.A.) in university and national life, the rapid growth of courses in religion and religious education in church and independent colleges, the development of schools of religion in State universities like the University of Iowa, and the official employment by some colleges and universities of chaplains and directors of religious activities and deans of religion— these are all aspects of a wider movement in American life for again bringing education and religion into closer partnership in national life.[1] There is a growing recogni-

[1] The best symposium on tendencies in religious life and movements in

tion that the struggle in the first three-quarters of the nineteenth century for public control of education was, in its secular aspects, aimed at the bitter sectarianism of the day and did not have at its heart the purpose of effecting as complete a divorce of religion (fundamentally conceived) and education as has taken place, particularly at the primary and secondary school level.

The American university with the undergraduate college at its heart has been looked at as a product of its own history. This history helps us to understand how it has become the kind of institution it is. That there are ludicrous elements in this system and much cultural thinness and superficiality no one can deny. But perhaps at the moment there is also substantial cause for hope for a more worthy university, because of the fearless and radical changes being made in all aspects of university life, sponsored as they are by all types of institutions, but especially by those leading universities, the practices of which have in other years so profoundly influenced American higher education.

American higher education is *Religion in Higher Education*, edited by Milton Towner, University of Chicago Press, 1931.

The University in the Fascist State

By ODDONE FANTINI

(Professor of Political Science in Perugia University.)

SHORTLY after the great educational reform in Italy had been achieved by Fascism, Mussolini declared in unequivocal terms that this was the most revolutionary of any of the reformations brought about by the Fascist Régime—revolutionary in the sense that it adhered more closely than any other to the spirit and ideals of the Fascist Revolution. But could this reformation be classed as reactionary and absolutist? Assuredly not, as it was one in which the spirit of Liberty predominated, in the elementary and secondary schools as well as in the university.

Fascist university reform is inspired by a realization of the necessity for freedom of the spirit in the domain of culture and science, if these are to find their fulfilment. The fundamental idealism which determined the genesis, establishment, and development of Fascism—idealism being understood not so much as a definite philosophical doctrine but as a profound spiritual necessity of life—has been the inspiration of this rebirth of the Italian university. Truly a problem pregnant with difficulties.

The reorganization and general ordering of the universities in Italy is a vexed problem going back for almost a century, and has a direct connexion with the glorious tradition of the

Italian universities throughout the Middle Ages and the Renaissance. Legacies are often cumbrous, and particularly those of great magnificence. The medieval universities were centres of culture, radiating light and wisdom throughout Italy and the whole world. For nearly six centuries, from the thirteenth to the eighteenth, the intense and fertile work of the Italian masters made possible a striking progress in all branches of study—law, letters, philosophy, physical science, biology, mathematics, philology, and history. It may be said without presumption that the history of this progress or, in other words, the history of these universities has played an important part in the unfolding of the civilization of Europe and the world. How were such results possible of achievement? Pre-eminently owing to the liberty enjoyed by both teachers and scholars.

The weight of tradition, which might appear to have been a negative influence in the development of some medieval schools, especially those of jurisprudence, has in reality always been counterbalanced by the vigilance of great masters able to reconcile it with the urgent claims of history and culture, and with the liberty, doctrine, and wisdom inherited principally from Rome. Thus has it been possible to raise that great monument of culture created by the free and glorious universities of Italy.

Paradoxical as it appears, it was in the very moment of realization of the nationalistic dreams of the great patriots, at the end of the Risorgimento when Italy finally redeemed her liberty, that the university relinquished the autonomy and liberty which it had until then so jealously guarded.

This was due to various changes in ideals and politics which greatly influenced the Italian spirit and institutions. As a matter of fact the liberty for which Italians fought for half a century, and which was to have been the supreme aim of their lives, was almost entirely neglected and forgotten immediately after the constitution of United Italy; and even as Italian life after 1860 was dominated by a monotonous indifference to the development of political forms and precepts, so in the universities—which, thanks to the unquenchable Italian spirit, were still able to produce masters—static regulations, liberal only in name, confined liberty within definite inflexible limits. The great ideal of liberty, applied not merely to politics, but to the organization of education and of the universities, which alone can produce real culture, productive science, teachers and scholars and great patriots, such as Bertrando Spaventa, Silvio Spaventa, Camillo Cavour, Cesare Balbo, and Raffaello Lambruschini, was frustrated for many years. A rigid and monotonous discipline was imposed on the universities by the law of 1859, which fixed uniform programmes, rules, and regulations, and the only liberty remaining was that which is in the hands of any teacher, namely, of striking at the heart of the nation by the diffusion of anti-national and subversive theories.

The problem, seen at its worst immediately after the Great War, made itself felt in the whole political, moral, civil, and religious life of Italy. Many notable men, anxious for the future of the universities, brought forward plans for reform which, regardless of party, were invariably based on the integral application of the principle of liberty in the regulations and activities of the universities. The most persistent of all the proposed reforms was that which was eventually carried out by Giovanni Gentile under the aegis of Mussolini in 1923, immediately after the constitution of the Fascist Government, and it has been the means of the realization of all the fundamental ideals which inspired and achieved the Fascist Revolution.

.   .   .   .

The basis of the university reform of 1927 was above all the restoration of absolute liberty—educational and administrative, spiritual, and scientific. The old order by which subjects, examinations, and time-tables were uniformly fixed for all the universities, was replaced by a new ordering calculated to create a living school, bent on stimulating unobstructed research, and founded on the idea of the university as a seat of the creation of culture and the formation of values.

As a first move, therefore, every university was given the most complete autonomy in teaching. To-day every university in Italy, without fear of outside interference, draws up its own statutes, which are scrupulously observed. In fact each faculty in a university is autonomous and makes its own regulations. For instance, it is interesting to note that to-day it is not easy to find two faculties of medicine, law, letters, or political science which employ the same methods and subjects. The autonomy, therefore, is complete in every way.

This autonomy is without doubt furthered by the fact that the administration is also independent. The universities are divided into three large groups—those completely controlled by the State; those controlled in part by the State and in part by other bodies (to these first two groups the Royal Universities belong); and those which are under the control of bodies other than the State, namely, the Free Universities. Each university has its own Board of Administration which leads to a marked cultural and didactic individuality. In fact, in the Italy of to-day the university has in great part returned to its glorious tradition of freedom for each institution to develop what scientific activities its financial and other possibilities allow, and to establish its own internal government. This naturally gives rise to a good deal of competition between the faculties of the different universities, which vie with each other in pedagogical methods and in obtaining highly qualified teachers, while the students on their side are free to choose whatever university they prefer.

This is a situation clearly favourable to a more rapid

advance of culture. Fascism has fully realized the importance of education of the mind and considers higher education as the means of revivifying science and personal values. An attempt has been made to exclude every material aim by giving no professional value to the degrees, although the professions are always kept in mind in planning the studies.

In the report accompanying the text of the reform it was stated:

'The fact that the University is intended as a seat of higher culture does not mean that it must or can ignore the professions. This would clearly be absurd. Its aim is, rather, apart from scientific progress, to furnish the necessary scientific culture for the exercise of the professions. It is essential, however, that this preparation for the professions offered by the University should be understood as a purely scientific education, so that degrees and diplomas have the exclusive value of academic qualifications. In order to exercise a profession it is necessary to pass State examinations in which only those who hold the relative academic degrees may take part.'

It is true that the criticism has been made that the opinions formed by students of a given university differ very greatly from those of the State Examination Board. These differences, however, do not affect the value of the reform. Fascism has never claimed to be infallible, nor does it with regard to the university, but with the experience gradually acquired it has been able to modify various laws and regulations. It has thus been possible to revise the whole system of nomination and choice of professors. These nominations are now made by a commission composed of five members chosen by the Minister, from amongst fifteen candidates proposed by the faculties concerned. The Faculty which has opened the competition has then the right to make its final choice from the three picked by the commission, so that here also a maximum of liberty is guaranteed.

In this respect the greater importance assumed by the system of private teaching in the Italian university should be noted. This, which used to be a glorious tradition of Italian higher education, has once more come into its own, though the fact that the official authorization to lecture privately is no longer necessary to the holding of a Chair, has somewhat detracted from its importance, It is, however, held in great honour in the important universities and the students make good use of it. To the students the private lecturers offer valuable co-operation both in scientific preparation and in their careers and the young men naturally derive great benefit from this close touch.

This does not mean that there is no contact between students and the official professors. On the contrary one of the principal aims of the reform was to achieve a real spiritual co-operation between teachers and students, with particular consideration for the point of view of the latter, and it is, in fact, to the student that the reform is particularly useful and adapted.

The old method of compulsory examinations, subjects, and regulations has been replaced by a free choice of subjects and methods of study, in accordance with the student's own leanings.

The Italian university is, in fact, a school of culture animated by the highest ideals, which inspire both its work and its ends.

.   .   .   .

The dominating influence, then, in the Italian universities is the principle of Liberty; it determines their whole mode of being.

What is the meaning, the value of this principle? Liberty, according to the Fascist doctrine, implies a complete independence of spirit and the development of ideals in all their potency. It includes the recognition of a religious exigency ever present in the depths of the human soul. It is activity and plenitude of the spirit and creation of values. It is the knowledge of human values, the sense of Life itself in all its ethical realization. Fascism values this liberty to the full and holds it of the greatest importance in politics, economics, and spiritual activities. Life which lacks liberty is without meaning; without liberty there *is* no life, no humanity, no ethical reality, but with liberty comes the ordering of the whole of life—political, juridical, economic, and cultural—because if it is true liberty it is at the same time duty and right, direction and limit, creation and the ordering of that same creation. Liberty creates for the joy of creating and not of destroying. It is religion itself, it believes, wills to believe, and knows it must believe in order that it may feel the supreme joy of labour which is realized in civil, social, economic, and moral relations. Liberty which does not create is nothingness; it is the negation of society. But unrestrained liberty is no longer religious and no longer moral. Liberty in the Fascist sense is the will to strive and create, the realization of faith and duty, and the right inherent therein. The liberty of democracy was egoistic, false, and materialistic, contrasting the individual with the mass, and particular interests with the world in general. Fascist liberty considers the individual as an ethical and universal reality, gifted with the greatest possibilities and initiative, but limited by this universality and ethical nature.

From this arises the conception of that State within which it is possible and necessary to concede the greatest political, civil, and economic liberty, but a liberty which is creative and not destructive. The old idea of a disintegrating liberty is opposed by the new one of a consciously creative liberty which constructs through belief in the State and Nation, in religion and the supremacy of spirit. Hence follows the interpretation of political life and economic and legal

relations as duty and ethics; hence the significance and value
of liberty in education and the reform of the universities
based on the principle of maximum liberty.

The complete understanding of this principle therefore
brings with it the realization of the tremendous constructive
power of the spirit, of culture as expansion of and intense
search after truth and as the greatest possible widening of
the boundaries of man's creative activity. In this light the
great democratic value of the reform of the universities is
seen at its noblest, democracy being understood not as
numbers, not as the individual opposed to the mass, nor as
the materialistic brutality of force, but as a more expansive,
elevated, profoundly human rendering of culture, drawing
its life from the springs of the spirit; not confined within set
limits, but freed from every obstruction and raised to a higher
level; regarded as the development of humanity and as a
spiritual force turned towards creation and towards ends
which are universal in the vastest sense and are, therefore,
above all nationality; which influence the spiritual life of
the world and make themselves part of international culture
and science.

.   .   .   .

The reform of the universities has also an obvious value
in the advance of learning. It is an old maxim that learning
is only possible under conditions of freedom, and the Italian
university is now placed in ideal circumstances for the fullest
development of learned research. It is a problem which has
been acutely felt for some years. In spite of often unfavour-
able financial conditions, extraordinary efforts have been made
and are being made by the laboratories and schools, which
constitute the centre of the nation's activities in this line,
to raise the level of grants for research purposes. During
late years there has been a rebirth of learned activities in Italy
such as could never have been conceived in the past. Societies

and institutes have been founded, national competitions organized, and new researches have once again placed Italian learning in the forefront, as has been proved in the recent national and international congresses.

Never have conditions in Italy been so favourable to the development of these activities as at the present time. Mussolini is their confident and enthusiastic promoter. He is the instigator of the new attitude towards research study, and all the societies, institutes, and foundations for research have been inspired by him; it was he who instigated, also, the reorganization of the university, which may be considered as cardinal for the new orientation of learning. Italy has made notable progress in recent years in all branches of learning—historical, philological, philosophical, religious, biological, astronomical, physical and moral. For the spirit of Fascism is imbued with the ideal of establishing Italy as a brilliant example of concrete realization of a higher civilization, whose beacon-light may shine forth to all nations in accordance with the ideal of international collaboration in science and culture which is the aim of Fascism.

Apart from this, however, it is only natural that Italian learning to-day should feel the duty of fulfilling a peculiarly national mission. The particular economic conditions of the country and the lack of many raw materials result in the greater part of scientific energy being directed towards essentially practical ends in line with Italy's particular requirements. Here also Mussolini has taken the lead. The many appeals he has made for the special study of whatever may be of direct or indirect aid to the development of national economic production are of great significance, and the Italian university has responded to his call with extraordinary enthusiasm.

This does not imply that the university and science in

Italy work for solely nationalistic ends. Despite Mussolini's appeal for a more historical interpretation of learning, and a close contact with the needs of life and of the nation, it is evident that it cannot be confined to national interests alone, but goes beyond, adapting itself to the necessities of science and culture throughout the world.

The whole conception of Fascism is to be understood, without reservation of any kind, as nationalism, both political and cultural, and it constitutes the powerful mainspring of all contemporary Italian life. For Italians and Fascists, however, nationalism does not stand for blind egoism, isolation from or opposition to other nations, but rather for a strong effort to make of the nation a vital centre of light, justice, and wisdom among the nations.

. . . .

A vast campaign for the reorganization and strengthening of technical and professional instruction is being carried out in relation to the economic life of Italy and an ever-increasing practical development of individual activities towards concrete ends. More has been achieved in this field during the last few years than ever before. Italy, saturated as she was with classical and artistic culture, had apparently never appreciated the enormous benefit to be derived from definite technical and professional instruction, which provides trained agriculturists, men competent to handle the big economic and financial questions which to-day more than ever weigh upon all the nations, and specialists in all branches of industry and production. All that has been done in this line is indicative, both from the political and moral view-points, of the enormous efforts which Italy is making to establish herself in a firm technical-economic position. Since 1922 nearly 500 legislative measures have been passed touching technical instruction. All the nautical and naval institutes, commercial schools, higher institutes for economic and commercial science, industrial and professional schools, have been reorganized and training schools have been opened; agricultural instruction has assumed great importance under the Fascist Régime.

One idea that pervades all this reorganization is that of unifying the control of education. Until recently the greater part of the institutes and technical schools were dependent on whatever central authority seemed best adapted to control their several activities. Now, all these institutes and schools have been placed under the direction of the Ministry of Education. Education in Italy, therefore, represents a clear and definite system, promoting the greatest development of the energies of the people in relation to the particular historical, political, economic and technical needs of the nation, and based on the Fascist conception of civilization. From this arises the national interest in all educational matters and the constant vigilance, care, and control exercised by the State.

.   .   .   .

The activities of the Italian university are, in fact, controlled by the State, within certain legal limits, and the State, having strengthened its authority particularly over those directly and exclusively dependent on it, has assumed the right of nominating the rectors and, with their assistance, the presidents of the various faculties. The oath of allegiance has been made compulsory for the professors, whose function is looked upon in relation to the moral and spiritual aims of the nation. This might appear to be a virtual suppression of liberty, but in fact it strengthens rather than weakens the freedom of the university. From a practical view-point the supervision of the State never goes beyond the limits set for it by the law and is perfectly compatible with the administrative and educational autonomy which has been granted to the university. It is also clear that the interest of the State in supervising the whole of university life is based on that very idea of liberty. Liberty, as we have said, and as the Fascist theory insistently proclaims, does not consist in the right to destroy the very creations of liberty nor in breaking down the ideals of the country, the nation, and the State. This would not be liberty, but its degeneration. The very logic of the Fascist State compels an ever-closer touch between the activities of the individual and the national life; in this respect university education is of paramount importance. In the university of the past it was possible to plot against the State and to conduct militant and party propaganda, the university thus failing to achieve its ultimate function of higher education. This does not occur any longer in Italy.

This does not mean, however, that higher education to-day adheres entirely to the spirit and ideals of the Fascist Régime. Contrary to the general supposition, and against the judgement of a large section of Fascists, the teaching in the university is carried out in an atmosphere of great liberty—always within the limits of the law and the spirit of the oath required from the professors. The nation is no longer betrayed by poisonous injections of corrosive theories, but on the other hand an orthodox Fascist teaching is not compulsory, and there are still many ideas which are not at all Fascist. Membership of the groups of Fascist professors is entirely voluntary and it is not uncommon to find actual opposition of ideas amongst the teachers of juridical and political subjects in the same university. It is generally the students themselves who pass judgement on these differences by deserting, as is their right, the classes of the non-Fascist professors. The whole problem, however, is not yet solved, though it has been much discussed of late years.

It would be ridiculous to suggest that the university should be non-political. Actual facts prove that the universities are centres of political life throughout the world, and this is especially true of Italy. For instance, the students strongly influenced the struggle for national independence, and again in 1915 they were a decisive factor in the declaration of the War, in which they gave themselves as officers in their tens of thousands to the cause of Victory. The students have also contributed and do contribute very greatly to Fascism; in fact the 'Fascist University Groups', which are directly dependent on the Fascist Party, embrace almost the entire mass of students and are a living force of the Régime.

As regards the content of university teaching, however, the political problem is not yet solved. The question is whether things should be left as they are or whether exceptional remedies are necessary. The prevalent opinion is that present teachers should continue to hold their positions regardless of party, but that in the course of the normal and gradual substitutions which must take place account should be taken of the political opinions of the new teachers. There are important arguments against this method; there is on the one hand the responsibility of the Régime in forming the new generation of Italians, especially those who, issuing from the higher schools, are destined to occupy positions of national importance; on the other hand there is the need of continually perfecting the Fascist doctrine and of completing the political reform of the universities. The gradual method has, however, been adopted. The universities have been subjected to a unified discipline, but no substantial changes have been made with regard to the teachers. Taking advantage of the elasticity of the university programmes, new Chairs have been instituted dealing with the new Fascist studies. A Faculty of Fascist Political Science has been created at Perugia in the heart of Italy, and other schools and faculties have arisen in various other centres for qualifying boys for public careers. Apart from these innovations there has been little change in the staffs of the universities, as it has been desired to avoid damage to scientific education by the possible substitution of teachers insufficiently prepared. There is also the feeling that on the whole the university is not antagonistic to the Régime, and that a system may gradually be perfected which will produce teachers capable of offering both a political and moral education and scientific instruction. When this programme is realized the university will respond in full to the faith which the Régime has rightly placed in it, a faith which was voiced by Mussolini already in 1923 in a speech to university professors and confirmed by him last year when he received a deputation of the National Association of University Professors, which society is dependent on and has its head-quarters in the National Fascist Party.

. . .   .

Altogether the Italian university is moving towards a substantial transformation based on ideals which Fascism intends to be fully achieved. The reorganization of 1923 corresponds in great part to the Fascist ideas of liberty in higher education, and to their firm desire to raise the moral and cultural, spiritual and scientific, standards of the nation. The university in Fascist Italy is working for the development of the personality and character of youth. Fascism is not an ordinary political party, but a special attitude towards life; an ideal system, not political alone but civil, moral, and religious, seeking a full realization. It is, in fact, the formation of new classes and new generations which will assure the continuance and potency of the Fascist Revolution. The whole educational system is founded on these ideals. It is desired to create a definite type of Italian, 'the Italian of Mussolini', whose character and personality must be perfectly adapted to the ideal and practical necessities of Italy, for which he will shape, by his own faith and tenacity of purpose, an independent future, dignified and sufficient for her moral and material needs.

Owing to this new outlook, men's whole attitude towards education has undergone a radical transformation. The change of name and the added attributes granted to what was the Ministry of Instruction and is now the Ministry of National Education is significant in itself. Fascism is convinced that education *per se* is sterile if not accompanied and supported by a faith and ideal, and that education includes and is more than instruction. Instruction is of the mind, education of the mind and spirit. This was also the conviction of the great educationists of the last century who urged the necessity of forming the character of the Italians for the new and greater Italy. Having made the country for the Italians, it was necessary to make Italians for the country.

Hence the great upheaval which has transformed the whole field of Italian education, including higher education. The interest of the nation is concentrated on this movement, as it is during the years of education that the character is definitely formed. It is this that necessitates the State control which, while leaving the greatest freedom in administrative matters, keeps careful watch that the true mission of the school be not betrayed. The Italian State in fact has always upheld its absolute right to have the last word in education, while allowing the universities as much independence as possible. The Catholic University of Milan, for instance, has its being and carries out its highly ideological programme according to the doctrines of the Church, but it is none the less watched and controlled by the Italian State.

The essential thing is, therefore, to make of the University a school for the formation of the character and spirit of the youth of the nation—of the personality of the New Italian. Personality is the basis of the historical and ideological interpretation of Fascism, for the Italy of to-morrow and of the dreams of the forebears of the present Fascist generation, will be the fruit of the labours of the youth educated to-day on Fascist principles.

This, however, does not exclude a preoccupation with learning. It has already been emphasized that this has a vital bearing on the problem of staff, and it assumes even greater importance when we think of the students. There is no need to deny that Fascism is and means to be a complete doctrine of Life and the State, which must be understood and perfected, so that it is essential that the university should contribute to the development of this doctrine—that the professors should teach and the students understand it.

The teaching reform has created the most favourable conditions for this, and the Italian of to-morrow, the product of the university, will be a fervent disciple of the Fascist doctrine, who will render Italy worthy of the honour of the whole world by labouring for the good of the country and the progress of humanity.

The University in Soviet Russia

By ALEXANDER P. PINKEVITCH

(Professor of Pedagogy, formerly Rector of the
Second State University in Moscow.)

Higher Education in Russia before the Revolution

UNIVERSITY education began in Tsarist Russia in the
eighteenth century, when the development of industry,
the end of the feudal system, the establishment of relations
with Western Europe, created a need for well-trained
specialists able to deal with the problems resulting from the
new possibilities of industry and to serve the interests of the
ruling classes.

The oldest Russian institute of higher learning was the
University of Petersburg, which was founded in 1730 and at
which lectures were delivered by foreign scholars specially
invited for this purpose. But in 1790 the university was closed,
as there was no special need for this type of institution, and
because there existed already in Petersburg an Academy of
Sciences under whose auspices the university had been
established. The University of Moscow, founded in 1755,
has had the longest continuous history of all Russian universities. Its aims are more practical: the training of lawyers and
physicians. In 1802 a university was opened in Juriev (Dorpat), in 1804 another in Kazan, then one in Kharkoff, and
finally, in 1819, the University of Petersburg was reopened.
The first specialized technical and pedagogic institutes were
also founded in Petersburg: the Institute of Mining in 1774,

the School of Civil Engineering in 1810, the Technical Institute in 1828, the School of Construction in 1842, reformed
into an Institute of Engineering in 1882.

Several important institutes have also been founded in
Moscow: the Petrovsky School of Agriculture, the Institute
of Technology, &c. At the end of the nineteenth century a
further series of institutes of university standard were founded
in Petersburg (the Polytechnic), Kieff, Saratoff, and elsewhere.

Amidst all these institutes of higher learning, it must be
emphasized that the universities played a predominant role,
from the academic as well as from the social point of view.
They possessed as a rule the following faculties: law, medicine, physics and mathematics, history and philology. A few
universities had a faculty of Oriental languages. They were
generally organized on the Western (German) model, with an
elected Rector, a board of professors, and a senate. Their
internal life was regulated by university statutes, established
successively in 1804, in 1835 (this statute limited the original
independence which they had been granted on the German
model), in 1863 (a more liberal statute), 1884 (which suppressed their right to elect their own rector and their own
professors).

In the period round 1905 the professors reflected the
opinions of the liberal *bourgeoisie* and the universities were
demanding new 'liberties' and their own autonomy. In
August a provisional ordinance was passed, granting them
their right to elect the Rector and the deans of the
faculties. But in general it can be said that the statutes of
1884 with various amendments were in force until the
October Revolution. In the closing year of this period university professors, who belonged mainly to the moderate
bourgeois parties, did not play any outstanding role in the
revolutionary movement. There were exceptions, and from

time to time there were incidents between the liberal party
of university professors and the Government, such as took
place in 1911 in the University of Moscow. The mass of
students were on the whole more active, but after taking an
important part in the revolution of 1905 they remained,
relatively speaking, passive during the two revolutions of
February–March and of October 1917.

An analysis of the social origins of the university class in
pre-revolutionary days shows a more or less complete absence
of representatives of the peasant or working classes. Out of
a thousand students there would be only a handful from the
village or the factory. The sons of merchants, industrialists,
the clergy, the gentry, men in liberal careers and in the Civil
Service—these went to the university. But in spite of the fact
that they all belonged to the Russian *bourgeoisie*, they were
violently divided in their political tendencies. One section,
belonging to the intellectual class which was itself a part of
the *petite bourgeoisie*, sympathized with the working classes;
others were interested in the peasants; others shared the convictions of the active bourgeois parties. Women students
were few. In the beginning they were not admitted at all.
Later, when they were granted the right to higher education,
access to the university was made so difficult that it was impossible for the majority to avail themselves of it. After 1905
they were again excluded until 1916, the eve of the revolution.

To complete the picture of pre-revolutionary Russian universities one must add that there were no 'national' universities or institutes for the different peoples living within the
frontiers of the Russian Empire. Certain culturally less
developed national minorities were in fact excluded from
higher education. The Jews were subject to a *numerus
clausus*.

The teaching given in the universities conformed, it is
needless to say, with the opinions and interests of the ruling

classes, the gentry, the landowners, merchants, and industrialists. The method of instruction was itself inspired by the ideology of the time, and the old dogmatic method of lecturing prevailed. If by any chance there appeared among the professors some who were dissatisfied with the condition of the university or who belonged to the liberal *bourgeoisie*, to the party of constitutional democracy or, in rare cases, even to the revolutionary parties, they had little chance of success and were, as a rule, forced to resign their positions. The history of Russian higher education is full of such examples, from the well-known mathematician Lobatchevsky to the historian Roshkoff. The latter, at the time of expulsion, was a member of the Bolshevist party. Such a situation excluded all liberty of scientific thought from among the professors as well as from among the students. Learning could only flourish *in spite of* the ruling régime, for it was inherent in the nature of this régime to be hostile to real knowledge. Higher education for women as a part of the general state system of learning did not at first exist. Such colleges for women as there were, were private enterprises. Medical training was first made available for them in 1872 with the opening of special courses at the Academy of Medicine and Surgery. The reactionary movement of 1882 had them closed. In 1872 also Professor Guerier organized university courses for women in Moscow; in 1876 courses of the same kind were organized in Kazan, and in 1878 similar courses in Petersburg and in Kiev. They included the following faculties: arts, history, physics, and mathematics. By the end of the century they had all been closed again, except the Bestoujeff courses in Petersburg. A fresh beginning was made by the revolution in 1905, and in the following years courses of university grade for women were established in Odessa, Kharkoff, Kiev, Warsaw, Dorpat, Kazan, Tiflis, Novotherkassk, and Tomsk. These courses included also agriculture, law, and medicine.

Higher Education after the October Revolution

The February Revolution did not bring any noticeable reform in the field of higher education. During the Provisional Government the organization and programmes of the universities remained the same. But after the October Revolution the situation changed. The Soviet Government and the revolutionary proletariat which took the place of the ruling classes reviewed with extreme care the inheritance which was left them by the old régime. They invited the co-operation of the professors. The Proletariat and its leaders of the Communist Party understood very well that the existing system of learning was full of elements hostile and harmful to the new régime, and that it was necessary to purge it of the bourgeois element with which it was permeated. But as they desired to keep all that was valuable in the bourgeois system the new rulers did not proceed to an immediate and violent destruction. The theory of the new government was often explained by Lenin. 'Proletarian culture', said he, when speaking at a congress of Communist Youth in 1920, 'must be the normal development of the reserves of knowledge which humanity worked out under the yoke of capitalist society, of the gentry and the bureaucracy.' The development of Science and higher education in the U.S.S.R. is an illustration and a practical realization of the statement of Lenin.

During the last fourteen years the higher educational system of the Soviets has passed through various phases. The first period lasted until 1921, when the first legislative measures were introduced. The second period lasted until 1928 and is a period of intensive reform, in the curriculum as well as in the organization of the university. Between 1928 and 1930 a complete reform of the whole field of higher learning was undertaken upon the basis of past experience. At the present time the main emphasis is the bringing of higher education into the closest co-operation with the needs of industrial production. As our chief interest lies in the present situation, only the principal features of the first three periods will be outlined in order to enable the reader to understand the path followed by Soviet higher education.

First Period (1917–21)

What was the situation of the universities the day after the October Revolution? For obvious reasons, neither professors nor students sympathized with the new régime. Both groups were closely bound up with the ruling class, with the capitalists. The situation is the same in all countries with capitalist governments. They obviously could not feel pleased that power had come into the hands of the class whose task was to destroy the *bourgeoisie* all over the world. At best they accepted the Soviet Régime as an unavoidable evil of a purely transitional character. They were convinced that it would not last long and that it had no firm roots. For this reason it is natural that there were a number of active counter-revolutionaries among the professors. Many fled or were banished. It is, however, only fair to bear in mind that some outstanding specialists among the Russian professors understood the significance of the revolution and decided to serve the Soviet Régime, and they are serving it faithfully up to the present time. But the trial of Chachtinsky in 1928 and the trial of the trade-group Ramsin & Co. are evidence that even among the 'loyal' professors there are irreconcilable enemies of the new régime. The Soviet power has done its best to win over scholars and men of science. Lenin was convinced that it was only possible to build up socialism immediately after the proletarian revolution by using elements belonging to the capitalist *bourgeoisie*, of which the intellectuals form a part. For these reasons he considered it necessary to grant to specialists and scientists the best conditions of life possible. 'This will be the best policy', he used to say, 'and the most economical way of ruling.'[1] The programme adopted at the Eighth Congress of the Communist Party in March 1919 also insisted upon the importance of obtaining the co-operation of bourgeois specialists, in a spirit of comradeship with the workers and under the guidance of the communists, in the common task before them. 'In this way manual and intellectual workers who had been divided by capitalism would be brought together in mutual understanding.'

In spite of the secret opposition of the professors and even of some of the students at the beginning of this period, important reforms were carried through. The universities at once became democratic. Access to them was made free to every one. No diploma and sometimes not even an examination was necessary for entrance, and women had equal rights with men. University autonomy assumed an entirely new form. At the head of the university was an elected Rector, at the head of each faculty an elected Dean; the elections were made not only by the professors and lecturers, but also by representatives of the students. In the period immediately following the revolution the students organized themselves independently into their own councils. But the Revolution scarcely affected educational matters. Lectures were delivered as before, and as before science was separated from production and practice.

Socially the students of this period remained the same as ever. They belonged to the small *bourgeoisie*, the bourgeois intellectuals, the former aristocracy, merchants, industrialists, and others. The number of students from the worker and peasant classes was small. The new régime took energetic measures to increase it; one of the most important was the

[1] Lenin, *Complete Works*, vol. xv, 1st edition, pp. 537, and vol. xvi, pp. 125 (Russian Original).

creation, in 1919, of 'workers' faculties', which was due to the initiative of a workers' quarter of the city of Moscow. These faculties accepted only workers from the factories and peasants from the villages and gave them a three years' training. They have proved of great value and are as significant to-day as ever. There is no question of reducing their number. Though it goes beyond the period under consideration, the following table shows the development of the workers' faculties in the Russian Socialist Federative Soviet Republic, which contains two-thirds of the population of the Union of Socialist Soviet Republics. For complete information it would be necessary to add the figures of other republics, but the table given is sufficient to show the development which has taken place.

Table of the development of Workers' Faculties from October 1st, 1919 to 1928–9.[1]

	Day Courses.	Evening Courses.	Joint Courses.	Total.	Total No. of Students.	Day-time.	Evening.
1919	3	—	—	3	2,149	2,149	—
1920	14	—	—	14	14,827	14,827	—
1921	40	4	1	45	30,224	30,224	—
1922	69	10	5	84	27,960	27,960	—
1923	53	4	8	65	30,035	30,035	—
1924	53	8	9	70	35,530	29,800	5,730
1925	44	8	13	65	31,664	25,500	6,164
1926	42	7	13	62	32,816	26,085	6,731
1927	40	7	15	62	33,238	26,085	7,153
1928	31	10	20	61	35,922	25,880	10,042
1929	32	14	22	68	38,380	27,025	11,355

Another important step taken by the Government was the increase in scholarships. The percentage of students receiving them was raised to 50. By 1931 a further 25 per cent. of

[1] See also pp. 193, 194.

students were in receipt of scholarships, and the amount of the scholarships had been increased from 100 to 200 roubles a month.

Second Period (1921–8)

This period opened with the drawing up of new regulations at a special conference on institutions of higher education held in the summer of 1921. These regulations were sanctioned by the Council of People's Commissars on July 3rd, 1922. The first paragraph of the new ordinance set forth the aims of higher education, which were

(*a*) to form specialists in the various branches of practical activity;

(*b*) to prepare scientists to work in the scientific, technical, and industrial institutions of the republic and in the institutions of higher learning themselves;

(*c*) to bring scientific knowledge to the proletariat and to the peasants, whose interests occupy the first place in the educational activity of the universities.

To be a student it was only necessary to be 16 years old, though later the age was put up to 17, and by 1931 to 18. It was characteristic of the new regulations that attendance at courses and lectures was open to every citizen of the required age. This meant that Soviet universities and institutes were open to every one in so far as the limitations of space in the laboratories permitted. Scientific workers were divided into three groups: professors who delivered independent courses, teachers who delivered supplementary courses, assistants who helped the professors and teachers. To-day the groups have been slightly changed. The professors have kept their title, the teachers are called lecturers, those who help the professors and lecturers, senior and junior assistants, and the new category of 'aspirants' has been added, viz. those who are preparing themselves for the career of scientific teaching.

The administration of the various institutions was entrusted to Boards, to be elected by a general assembly of all professors, teachers, and students. The list of nominees chosen by these three groups, and others chosen by the local administration, by economic and trade union organizations, were to be forwarded to the Commissariat for People's Education, which had the power of confirming their election. The new ordinance also contained a very typical decision: that the rectors appointed by the Commissariat must in all cases be chosen from a list submitted by the professors and teachers of the institutes concerned. The Board had full authority in all matters of administration, but the Rector retained the right of independent action if he deemed it necessary.

It was during this second period that radical changes in the function of the universities took place. Before the Revolution they included faculties of medicine, physics and mathematics, history and arts. After the Revolution the faculties were re-organized and the emphasis was put upon those of technology and pedagogy. The latter faculties have all been founded since the Revolution. Before that there were no true university courses for the training of teachers. As will be seen, the Soviet university thus presents various analogies with the American in its combination of Arts Courses with technical faculties.

This period was also characterized by the steady growth in the number of proletarian students. The following table is of interest:

	workers	peasants	functionaries	others	
1923–4:	15·3	23·5	24·4	27·8	per cent.
1927–8:	26·9	24·2	39·0	9·5	,,

In other words, by 1928 half of the students in the universities came from the worker and peasant classes, though the percentage naturally differed according to the university or institute concerned. In industrial and technical schools it was particularly high. It was small in the schools of arts. The women formed one-third of the total number of 160,000 students (of whom 120,000 are in the R.S.F.S.R.). This did not include the students of the Communist universities, whose aim is to prepare party workers and leaders in the Soviet System.

During these years a considerable development took place also in the professional unions and other organizations of intellectual workers. A special section for scientific workers was created in the general union of educationists. The end of this period marked the formation of a special Pan-Russian Association whose aim was to assist in the building up of the Socialist system and of the Communist Party. This organization is called, after the first letters of the words composing its official title, VARNITSO. There was further a development in student self-government, which, during this period, became one of the principal planks in university reorganization. The majority of students united into professional unions, similar to the trade unions, and corresponding to the unions of intellectual workers. A university might contain one union of medical workers, another of teachers, and a third of metallurgists. At the same time the curricula were reorganized and new methods of teaching introduced. Both students and professors were enthusiastic supporters of more active and direct methods of instruction. Seminars, laboratories, experimental schemes took the place of oral teaching and lectures.

Through the activity of the Institute of Red Professors and of the Communist Academy, and through the creation of the Institute for Aspirants, the number of teachers who were Communists or whose ideology was friendly to the Soviet Power was growing and the proletarization of higher education was slowly but inevitably being realized. The general situation, however, was still unsatisfactory. The special training was not yet vitally connected with industry or with the workers and peasants, in spite of the very important social work which each student did during his university year.

Third Period (1928–30)

A further change was inaugurated by a resolution of the Central Committee of the Communist Party on July 12th, 1928. This resolution stated that technical training was divorced from industrial production, that the practical side of industrial study was poorly organized, that the extraordinary length of the courses (six to eight years) in the engineering colleges constituted a tremendous handicap, and led as a direct consequence to only a few students finishing their studies. At the same time it was decided that the method of giving practical work in industry should be completely changed and that students should have a year's uninterrupted training in some industrial enterprise. The same resolution requested also the directors of trusts and industries to pay more attention to the engineering colleges and to exert an active influence in developing their methods of teaching. The resolution recommended the reconsideration of the curricula and the invitation of leading foreign specialists to give lectures and courses. It was suggested that the length of the course should be reduced to five or six years, including one year for practical work. But the most important decision taken was for the transference of six engineering colleges and five technical institutes to the control of the Supreme Economic Council, and of two technical institutes to the Commissariat of Means of Communication, though only in so far as their curricula and methods were concerned. Up to that time all institutes of higher learning had been united under the direction of the Commissariat for Public Instruction. By this new step the Central Committee of the Communist Party initiated a new form of administration, in that each institute was now related to its corresponding administrative body.

Several of these measures had already been anticipated by other decisions of the Central Committee of the Communist Party. But progress during the first year was slow. The continuous practical work, which corresponds to 'the American Co-operative Plan', was being realized on a very small scale. For this reason the Central Committee, in November 1929, reiterated its instructions. A further far-reaching reform was also resolved upon, and the length of courses was reduced to four and in some cases even to three years.

On the subject of continued practical work the resolution stated that 'it is necessary in the future to develop and to improve the practical work in industry of the students. From 40 per cent. to 50 per cent. of their time must be given to this. A proper balance between theoretical and practical training must also be established and adapted to the different branches of production. Practical work and theoretical instruction might alternate in monthly or longer periods according to the course.'

The Supreme Economic Council was asked to create one or two Institutes in organic connexion with factories, to serve as centres for practical work and production, and at the same time for the preparation of three grades of skilled specialists. Specialization along very narrow lines was thus introduced, but without excluding general technical education.

These resolutions introduced radical changes into higher education. Their main feature was the introduction of the period of uninterrupted practical work in industry. The student had previously gone into the factories and shops only for short periods, generally in the summer. But now there were continuous relations between the engineering colleges and the works throughout the year and the student spent half of his study years in paid positions in a factory. It is generally known that about twenty engineering courses in the United States have, owing to the initiative of Professor Schneider, adopted a similar plan. But in the U.S.S.R. every institution of higher learning had to include in its curriculum the period of uninterrupted practical work in production. Practical production and learning were thus in constant co-operation.

This reform called for a radical transformation of the old method of teaching and for a further reduction in the number of lectures. The system of laboratory groups assumed an ever-increasing importance, and the whole structure of higher education changed. The same was true of university administration. The regulations of 1921–2 were repealed. At the head of the university there was no longer a university board, but a director who was solely responsible for all that happened in the university, in exactly the same way as a director controls, and is responsible for, the work of a factory. The role of the student organizations was in no way diminished. The professional unions of intellectual workers maintained their importance. But in no case could responsibility be laid upon either of them.

Fourth Period (1930 *up to the present day*)

A government resolution of the beginning of 1930 introduced a further change of no less significance than that introduced in 1928–9 into the training methods of the university. Every institution of higher learning was attached to the corresponding administrative body or to an economic organization. Only pedagogical and social-economic institutes remained under the direct control of the Commissariat for Public Instruction. All the others were allotted to different administrations, to separate trusts and to economical associations. As a result of this decision several universities were divided into separate institutes. The second university of Moscow, for example, with its faculties of medicine, chemistry, and pedagogy, was divided into three units, each with the title of 'Institute'. The number of universities and technical institutes was also reduced. At present universities are still maintained in Moscow, Leningrad, Kazan, Saratow, Tiflis, Minsk, Tashkent, and a few other centres. Several universities remain temporarily unchanged. Those of Kazan and Saratow for instance will probably keep their title. In the Ukraine, from the very beginning of the Republican Government, the title 'university' has been maintained.

The few universities that still exist have the task of training specialists in literature, philology, arts, the humanities, physics, chemistry, and biology.

The purpose of all these tremendous reforms was to interest the competent authorities and economic organizations in a higher education whose immediate object was to prepare specialists. As a matter of fact, it is remarkable to note that as soon as education passed under the control of these bodies the number of institutes grew rapidly. Not so long ago there were in the R.S.F.S.R. seventy institutes of higher learning. To-day there are 300, and their total in the U.S.S.R. reaches 500. The number of students in higher education was:

in 1927–8 in the R.S.F.S.R. . . . 107,396
           ,,   U.S.S.R. . . . 159,774
in 1930–1   ,,   R.S.F.S.R. . . . 171,865
           ,,   U.S.S.R. . . . 271,961
in 1931–2   ,,   U.S.S.R. . . . 394,000
in 1932–3   ,,   U.S.S.R. . . . 548,000 (estimated).

The number of students in higher technical and professional schools (*technica*) was:

in 1927–8 in the R.S.F.S.R. . . . 128,923
           ,,   U.S.S.R. . . . 188,542

in 1930–1 in the R.S.F.S.R. . . . 352,536
    ,, U.S.S.R. . . . 609,064
in 1931–2 ,, U.S.S.R. . . . 855,000
in 1932–3 ,, U.S.S.R. . . . 970,000 (estimated).

The number of students in Workers' Faculties (Rabfacs) for U.S.S.R. was:

in 1930–1 229,000
in 1931–2 325,000
in 1932–3 . . . . 450,000 (estimated).

There is also intense activity in the study of method. The whole of the work is being reconstructed upon new principles. 'Outlines' are being elaborated to try to determine the ideal type of specialists for the new socialist economy and the cultural revolution. New curricula are being worked out based upon the problems of production and industrial practice. The decision taken by the Government on May 3rd, 1931, strengthens still further the practical work of the individual student. It provides that such students instead of receiving scholarships shall receive the salary corresponding to their work. The amount of this salary may not be less than the scholarship.

Part-time education and various correspondence courses are growing very rapidly. New teaching methods are also being elaborated.

Great attention is being paid to the organization of the learning process of students and the new system of study called the 'Laboratory Brigade Plan' is more and more in evidence. The Schools in organic connexion with factories are also very important and several have already been created.

Considered as a whole the progress made by higher education in the U.S.S.R. has all been directed towards the bringing of higher education into line with the building up of a socialist society and with the interests of the working classes, the peasants and the co-operative rural organizations. The socialist industrialization of the entire economic system of the country, the development of collectivization, the foundation of huge enterprises in the field of industry and rural economy, all this created the need for a tremendous number of specialists, specialists of a new kind, possessing a full knowledge of the latest achievements in technical science, and at the same time devoted heart and soul to the working classes and to the socialist reconstruction of our country. The need for skilled workers is indeed tremendous. The rate of progress achieved by the various branches of socialist reconstruction during the past years shows clearly that science and higher education have been lagging behind. But it is quite obvious that the training of specialists is one of our most urgent problems and an essential condition for the success of socialism in the U.S.S.R.

Never has the problem of higher education been so acute as it is now. There is immense activity in all the commissariats, which are elaborating study outlines, programmes, new methods of teaching. In the institutions themselves all the workers are burning with enthusiasm and with the desire to create a school which shall really correspond to the interests of the socialist system. The 16th Congress of the Communist Party has declared that the problem of the creation of leaders in the technical and economic field is the central problem of reconstruction. 'Only by a united mobilization of all the forces of the Party and of the working classes, for the solution of the problem of training leaders from among the working classes, will it be possible to maintain the speed of Bolshevism in the industrialization of the country.'

The enthusiasm with which the institutes for higher education are accomplishing this creative activity proves that the resolution of the 16th Congress of the Party has not been in vain. It is impossible to escape the conviction that the problem of specialized institutes as well as secondary schools will soon be resolved in the spirit of the revolutionary proletariat and in the interests of the Social revolution in Soviet Russia.

The Conception of a Catholic University[1]

By DR. DIETRICH VON HILDEBRAND

(Professor of Metaphysics and Ethics at the University of Munich.)

THE nature and conception of a university depend essentially and in the first place on the nature of true science and knowledge. It is therefore necessary to consider the fundamental problems which are the implicit presupposition of every university by its very nature, namely those concerning the nature of true knowledge, if we are to discuss the justification and value of a Catholic university and therewith to form a critical estimate of the present-day 'liberal' university.

The university of the present time rests on a fundamental principle, viz. that all apprehension and knowledge is an autonomous function of the human mind which is and must be independent of man's will, his moral constitution, his general philosophical, not to speak of his religious, attitude, if the knowledge is to lay claim to being adequate and objective. Two points require here to be distinguished: (*a*) the assertion that knowledge as such is independent of the general attitude of man; that is, that in its very structure it does not

---

[1] While the editors are themselves responsible either in whole or in part for the other translations in this book, they wish to express their warm gratitude to Mr. Edward Bullough of Cambridge for his admirable translation of Professor Hildebrand's article.

involve any other attitude of the person; and (*b*) that true knowledge must not, as far as its content is concerned, operate with any presuppositions other than those which can be justified before the tribunal of knowledge itself.

This second point has often been expressly formulated, and is what is meant by expressions such as 'freedom from bias or prejudice', 'absence of presuppositions'. The first point is usually assumed tacitly and implicitly. Reserving the second point for the moment, I turn to a critical examination of the first.

It is one of the profoundest and most characteristic traits of a spiritual personality to be able to make intellectual and spiritual contact with reality by apprehending its concrete quality and existence. The peculiar nature of a spiritual personality as consciously existing finds expression precisely in this capacity, and without this capacity a personal being would be unthinkable. A personality not only exists in a real causal relationship to surrounding things, but is also capable of coming into contact with them in this purposive manner, by, as it were, grasping them intellectually from above and by taking possession of them in the act of 'knowing' them.

There are many degrees within this knowledge or apprehension: from merely taking note of a thing up to an understanding grasp of its nature; from mere apperception up to an explicit theoretical penetration of its content and a systematic exploration of the extent of its being. Again, there are many kinds of apprehension according to the nature of the thing apprehended: as the perception of colour, the hearing of sounds, the appreciation of a value, the observation of a complex situation; and so there are many kinds of theoretical penetration, according to the special nature of the object and according to the nature of the problem, as, for instance, causal-genetic knowledge, historical knowledge, psychological knowledge, descriptive knowledge, and last but not least, philosophical knowledge. A scientific, theoretical apprehension presupposes in addition the merely pre-scientific perception of the thing, in most cases. What are the relations between apprehension or knowledge in the widest sense of that term and the general attitude of the person?

It must be expressly emphasized that all views which attempt to interpret the certitude resulting from apprehension of the existence or non-existence of a fact as an act of the will are wholly mistaken. On being apprehended, a thing is found to exist; the question of its existence or non-existence is decided by apprehension without interference on the part of the will, and the certitude, as a *theoretical* attitude to be kept clearly distinct from the *practical* attitude of the will, registers this decision on the part of the subject, or, in other words, gives the answer which the object demands. Any endeavour to represent the determination of the existence of a fact in apprehension as insufficient, or as requiring a supplementary act of the will, misses the real nature of knowledge. The determination lies within the region of apprehension itself; the object itself is decisive for the emergence of a conviction or certitude, *it* solves the question of its existence, *it* informs me, *it* proves itself and it leaves nothing to be supplied by an act of my will, as if the final certitude were completed by the will. Yet, even though we must reject every form of 'voluntarism', there are nevertheless so many connexions between the apprehension and the general attitude of a person, that it is equally impossible to isolate knowledge in a watertight compartment and to conceive the capacity of knowing as wholly neutral in regard to this general attitude.

For, even if knowledge considered in itself and in regard to what it presents, is autonomous, yet the capacity of knowing depends largely upon the general attitude of the person that knows. Defective general attitudes are very apt to close the intellectual eye and to darken its vision; the right attitude, on the contrary, confers sight. I merely call attention to the most elementary moral pre-requisites for an adequate apprehension: such as an honest desire for truth, absence of bias, thoroughness. It is evident that superficiality, frivolity, amateurish trifling, lack of thoroughness, dishonesty, prejudice—all of them factors which are not primarily qualities of the intellect, but of the character—fundamentally damage the power to know or the result of its apprehension.

But these are only the most obvious factors belonging to the moral sphere which influence apprehension. The history of errors, especially in philosophy, like materialism, pantheism, scepticism, psychologism, idealism, positivism, relativism, radical empiricism, &c., show clearly that there are far deeper connexions between the general attitude of man and his capacity of knowing, and that we have to begin with the fundamental forms of man's attitude in order to appreciate the full scope of the formal and material dependence of knowledge on the very nature of man.

Attitudes of Apprehension

I start with the *negative* attitudes which interfere with the capacity of apprehension.

There we find in the first place, *indolence*. I do not mean here that peripheral indolence which keeps man from any intellectual labour, 'laziness' so called, but I mean a much more central, I should like to say 'metaphysical', indolence of the mind which influences apprehension. I mean the indolence which renders any real penetration of the object impossible and prevents any collaboration with the meaning and essence of a thing. Certain kinds of things, which lie outside the normal visual field of a person, such as the nature of personality, the nature of value, of a given situation, and of essences, or the existence of certain spiritual complexes like 'epochs of civilization', or social organisms, like nations, or the existence of juridical facts, like treaties, &c., require for their apprehension a certain *élan* of the whole man, a kind of soaring-power of the mind, a willingness to abandon a customary attitude and to look in a new direction, and, above all, to allow oneself to be carried along by the spirit of the object in question and to 'collaborate', to 'conspire' with it. But this indolence, anchored deep down in the concupiscence of man, a *laissez-aller*, a strange dull insistence on remaining rooted to the spot one is accustomed to, close whole stretches of reality to the intellectual vision. As long as we remain in this attitude of central indolence, no intellectual acumen, no abundance of erudition, no merely formal capacity of apprehension can open our eyes to the understanding of the deeper strata and connexions of existing things, or of higher kinds of objects of knowledge. A typical instance of the result of an apprehension darkened by this attitude is materialism, which will allow only such things to exist as are presented in a quite definitive manner, namely within the *immediate* field of vision. To the same class belongs the 'Association-Psychology' inasmuch as it attempts to apprehend personality primarily with the principles of the material world; in the same class we must reckon, in fact, all attempts to reduce the Cosmos to a form of being which can be easily grasped, such as the system of Freud. In such cases, any advance in understanding must begin with a totally new general attitude of the man; for no effort of the understanding as such is capable *per se* of overcoming the error, as long as this metaphysical indolence persists. It is the same attitude which, in other spheres of life, we describe as that of the 'materialist'.

Another fundamental attitude darkening the understanding is the incapacity, which is rooted in *pride*, to listen, to let things themselves speak, to allow them to instruct us. What I mean here is that pedagogic pedantry in face of the World which destroys all θαυμάζειν, which, according to Plato, is the beginning of all true knowledge. There are people who approach things in their apprehension without the respectful desire to penetrate them with real understanding, without any 'thirst' for truth, but rather with a supercilious repletion and a Boeotian smugness which renders open-mindedness impossible. People of that kind are blind to many things even in their *pre*-scientific apprehension; *a fortiori* in their systematic knowledge; blind to all the things that constitute the height and the depth of the world. Even their *pre*-scientific picture of the world is flattened out and deformed by reduction in scale; so their scientific apprehension lacks the vision for differentiation, mystery, and the endlessness of things. However sagacious, however thorough and industrious in their research they may be, the result of their apprehension is permeated by errors. Of course, this darkening of their understanding affects different spheres of knowledge in different degrees; most fatally of all philosophy. But wherever it appears, it cannot remain without damaging consequences: think of history, psychology, medicine, law. A typical expression of knowledge disfigured by such schoolmasterly metaphysical pedantry is the explicit rationalism of the 'Age of Enlightenment'; so is the mania for superficial systems which bear no relation to actually existing things, force everything into a few miserable categories, and hasten to reduce all sorts of things which in their particular being constitute fundamental phenomena to something 'known', because such minds will not admit that 'there are more things in heaven and earth than are dreamt of in their philosophy'.

Worse still is the attitude of definite *resentment* which rebels against the objectivity and autonomy of things and especially against the existence of objective values. It resents being bound by an objective validity. It prevents any real 'making friends' with an object, any willingness to listen to the voice of things, and it does so, not as a conscious gesture, but—

much worse—as an unconscious fundamental attitude. It blinds the eye of the intellect towards the most patent truths, not so much to their material content as to their evidential value and to the objectively verifiable existence of contexts or their inner necessity, as for instance that a straight line is the shortest line between two points, or that twice two is four. This attitude prevents any illumination, because at bottom it does not want to be illuminated. This is the attitude of the radical sceptic, be he called Gorgias or otherwise, or that of the relativist who repeats with deep satisfaction the absurd thesis of the relativity of all values. In face of such minds no arguments are of the slightest use, however convincing they may be: they will not admit the convincing power of argument. Nothing but the abandonment of their fundamental attitude, only a 'conversion', a relaxing of the orgasm of their pride, can give them sight and lead to a liberation of their intellect. All the results of their knowledge are misled and misleading as long as this cramped pride is not relaxed, however sagacious, however 'clever' they may be, and however 'scientific' their methods. We may remember the world of Nietzsche's thought, in which the source of all his error and of his blindness to the true moral values is so clearly displayed in his fundamental attitude, or the tragic figure of Max Scheler, all of whose conclusions in his last anti-catholic period are so unambiguously inspired by his moral attitude. Perhaps it is precisely in the sphere of the apprehension of values that the blinding effect of such a false general attitude can most easily be detected, and the root of every blindness to moral values has to be sought in such an attitude.

Lastly, there is a fundamental attitude of lack of spirit, of *distrust* towards things, which disturbs the understanding and condemns it to impotence. I mean here that constitutional distrust which renders a man incapable of understanding the simplest set of facts, because he cannot muster the necessary courage to entrust himself to the object, and because it seems to him an act of rashness to reach a definite conclusion at any point whatever. Perpetually he refers the 'decision' to a further court of appeal, and avoids a definite 'yea' or 'no' even in the most patent situations. This attitude in the intellectual sphere corresponds in the moral sphere to the running away from every responsibility. I do not mean that in the intellectual sphere the final decision rests with an act of the will: this, as explained before, is not the case. The decision rests with the object; our will does not come in question. All the same we must open our minds and make contact with the object to the extent of being able to follow up this objective decision subjectively; but in the case of the metaphysical coward and doubter, it is precisely this necessary friendly contact with the thing, this having an 'open mind' with regard to it, that is lacking. With his preconceived distrust he avoids having anything to do with the thing lest it should inform him or give him the decisive answer, he as it were stops up his ears to it. The expression of this attitude is to be seen in an unmistakable tragic scepticism, especially in the ceaseless demand for a criterion, in the dislike of all intuition, in mistaking the highest and most evident connexions for artificially propounded axioms, in the distrust of all material understanding, in the preference for purely formal rather than material knowledge, in the tendency to regard illusion as normal (apperception as *hallucination vraie*), in the incapacity to distinguish between evident and non-evident facts, and in a false ideal of scientific accuracy and exactness.

True knowledge must be unprejudiced. It must not rest in its search upon facts which are incapable of withstanding the test of reason. Neither is true knowledge formally a function of the general attitude of man, as if the *result* of knowledge, instead of being given by the object, were rather the *object* of the apprehension itself or dependent on the will and attitude of the knower. Nevertheless the knower must assume the *right attitude* in order to grasp the thing as it is, to let it speak for itself without interference, to allow the understanding to proceed unhindered and to work itself out in its specific function without deformation or obstacle. A false attitude, just like inherent defects of the intelligence such as stupidity, muddleheadedness, or idiocy, deforms the power of apprehension and obscures its content. The right attitude, on the contrary, clears away all obstacles from the path of a full and pure exercise of the understanding and delivers knowledge from its fetters.

Now, the right attitude is precisely the opposite of metaphysical indolence, a certain winged alertness of the mind, peculiar to the humbly loving, reverent personality, in contrast to the merely concupiscent self. I mean here not a merely formal mobility of mind, a formal capacity for differentiation, which many possess who nevertheless lack all real contact with things, nor that intellectual agility which so easily turns knowledge into a sport and, without ever really collaborating with the objective world, turns intellectual somersaults, that formal nimbleness which the sophists possessed in so high a degree and the unphilosophical world rejects as sheer 'dialectics'. I mean rather that quite consciously directed alertness of a man which enables him to be emotionally affected by all genuine values, to surrender himself with affection and good-will to all real goods, 'to keep step' and to 'conspire' with the object of his understanding. I mean the general resonance of the mind which makes man free, which produces a response to value in the moral sphere instead of eternally seeking for pleasure, and in the intellectual sphere implies following the cue given by an object, being led by it, being able to vibrate in unison with its *ratio*—the contrast to 'stick-in-the-mud' laziness, the antithesis to all dullness. The right attitude is further one of reverent yet loving open-mindedness, in opposition to the schoolmasterly pedantic superciliousness. The same reverent attitude which, in the moral sphere, produces the yearning to participate in the world of values, and especially in God, yields in the intellectual sphere the 'thirst for truth', the desire to participate by understanding in the world of existents; the metaphysical open-mindedness of a man who desires to 'receive', who will not prescribe to Nature *his* laws, who is willing to listen to the Universe and to the wealth of its mysteries. It is that attitude which St. Bonaventura means when he says at the opening of his *Itinerarium mentis ad Deum:* 'These things can be understood only by one who is, like Daniel, a man of desire'; a willingness to 'become empty', the power to keep silent and to let things speak for themselves. It is a reverence filled with the awareness of the depth and wealth of the Cosmos, which rejects all pedantic violence done to it, which approaches things with the readiness to do justice to the profundity of things—the very contrast to the familiar 'chumming-up' with the Universe—and an inner willingness to be subordinate and to serve.

This attitude in no way prejudges the content of understanding in particular cases. It merely 'liberates' the understanding, creates the conditions requisite for the full development of objective apprehension and renders it in the fullest sense unprejudiced. An understanding resting upon this attitude does not by any means 'romance' enthusiastically about things; no—it alone, by reason of its open-mindedness and selflessness, is capable of understanding anything in its own peculiar essence: great things in their greatness, small things in their smallness, simple things in their simplicity, differentiated things in their complexity, a whole in its wholeness, independent parts in their autonomy, the sublime in its sublimity, sanctity in its own singular mysteriousness—

because it alone allows the object to speak for itself, which is after all the nature and soul of all true understanding. The attitude which, so to say, makes understanding a gift to itself, is moreover reverent in contrast to frantic pride and all resentment against things. It is a liberated inner freedom, which, not rebelling against truth, does not feel the existence of objective truth as an oppression and restriction, but as liberating and rejoicing. Again, it means the inner willingness which is not closed against even the most unpleasant truth, which is really free from bias, ready to make friends with things, open to the proof of all objective existence, not looking at things through a coloured lens which allows only such things to pass into the understanding as do not offend our pride and our self-complacency.

And finally, this attitude which permits understanding to develop without prejudice, is also that of metaphysical courage and faith. It is willingness to embark upon the great venture of letting oneself be carried along by things, a simple, sane, intellectual readiness to listen to their voice. The same attitude which will not shirk moral responsibility will also meet things without the prejudice of distrust which dims the vision for evidence and for the differences between what is and what is not evident. It is an unbiased, trusting attitude which does not render man uncritical or gullible, but merely enables him to take that step, essential to understanding, which creates a real contact with things, moves with them, opens to them the intellectual eye and ear. Just as the man obsessed with scruples moves in a perpetual circle and no longer understands the clear voice of conscience, no longer perceives the difference between good and evil, between what is and what is not permitted, so does the constitutional coward and sceptic in knowledge. For there exists the type obsessed by scruples in understanding, and he, so far from being more exact, more thorough, or more critical than the trusting man, is, on the contrary, less objective, less thorough, and less critical. For all exactness and critical reserve presuppose the clear distinction between what is and what is not evident; the uncritical attitude consists precisely in *not* grasping this difference, and it is just as uncritical to deny from constitutional distrust the evidence of proof, as carelessly to consider unproven truths as evident.

Deformation of the Understanding

Before dealing with the influence of Religion on this liberating attitude of the individual, I want shortly to sketch a few typical, but constitutional deformations of the understanding, serious generic errors which, in affecting the content of knowledge, have their repercussions in darkening the vision of the mind and permeate the whole understanding and conduct—errors typical of certain classes of men and falsifying fundamentally their picture of the world.

Here we find, first of all, what I should like to call an 'eidetic' blindness. The person suffering from this defect lacks the vision for the real features of things, for their 'eidos', for what is essential and significant in a thing, in distinction from all accidental and secondary features of the concrete specimen. This class is represented by men who conceive the step from the concrete thing to what is generic or typical merely as a reduction to the average, incapable as they are of grasping the immanent significance of a thing, that which it tends to embody; they mistake the permanent average for what is essential and typical. They are faced with the simple but false alternative: *either* the concrete thing with all its accidental features (further confusing incidentally the accidental features as essential with the really constitutive and essential elements), in other words, an unintelligent statement of the material fact viewed merely from outside; *or* a generalization obtained from a statistical average, a mediocre, anaemic, and mechanical pattern. They operate with a false conception of truth and reality: they *either* take the isolated specimen in its undifferentiated accidental being, without understanding its significance and immanent ideal, to be the only existing reality, and consider the significance of a thing, the thought of God embodied in it, as a mere phantasm, or confuse it with the threadbare, bloodless, artificial, unreal, abstract pattern; or—*per contra*—they consider the average pattern as the true thing and arrive at a typically pedantic schoolmasterly violation and deformation of the wealth of all things.

We need but remember the identification in medicine of the concept of health with the 'average case' or the theory of Lombroso concerning genius and insanity, which regards everything deviating from the average as abnormal without distinguishing between a more fully realized ideal exceeding the average and a falling short of the ideal. Such men mean by common sense the average form of a *pre*-scientific reflection, instead of regarding it as the classical aspect of the Cosmos as found in immediate naïve experience. They are incapable of grasping either form or meaning and consider all these distinctions in history and psychology as artificial quibbles. They propose to deal with the history of art without any sense for art and without taking the value of the work of art into account. They are afraid that to go beyond a dull statement of fact or arid statistics means leaving the *terra firma* of reality. They pursue biology without seeing the living thing, psychology without grasping personality, sociology without understanding the essence of community-life. In philosophy they are without feeling for the world of essences, for the *a priori*, and cling to a dreary empiricism. They hope to apprehend reality, approaching it wholly from outside, with the help of experiment and statistical information and the collection of material data, and deride in their helpless blindness all analysis of essences as idle dreams. They consider their very blindness as a sturdy sense of reality: the lower a thing is in the order of existence the more reliable it seems to them; an instinctive act appears to them as more real, as more solid than an act of the mind. In ethics they try to deal with morality on the basis of the 'success' of behaviour without even discussing the qualitative difference of 'good' and 'evil'. In art they are aware only of the alternative between a dreary Naturalism with its slavish copying of accidental, unessential detail, with its studio-atmosphere, its undressed persons instead of nudes—or, on the other hand, an equally dreary classicism and a mechanical, artificial, pale idealization.

In life they are incapable of penetrating to the deeper layers of things, they boast of the pseudo-realism of the 'practical' man, of a false common sense, incapable as they are of freeing themselves from the trivial alternative: the so-called 'realist' v. the so-called 'idealist'. In the one they see a man with a sense for the 'realities' of life, often a mere clinging to the most obvious externalities of it; in the other an 'idealist', that is a dreamer (or, as they prefer to call him, 'a mystic'), blissfully unsuspecting that the mystic is precisely he who, bursting through the fetters of this whole pedantic alternative, is nearest of all to true reality, nearest to the *ens realissimum*, God. They are the Boeotians who consider the economic sphere as the real and only serious aspect of life, while they consider knowledge, art, love, as mere luxuries.

A second generic deformation of knowledge is the false ideal of 'amplitude', if I may use that expression. It is a formalistic blindness. What I mean is the confusion of amplitude with the formal range of a concept. This type fails to grasp qualitative amplitude, the amplitude which the higher value possesses, because it contains *per eminentiam* the lower. A person of this class will consider an object as wide in proportion as it lacks definition; he confuses infinity with

indefiniteness. He harbours, in consequence, a curious resentment against all material knowledge, because it narrows
him down and oppresses him. Purely formal knowledge
seems to him more distinguished, purer, freer. In ethics
he confuses concrete ethics with casuistry; abstract ethics
strikes him as grander, less fettered. His religion is pantheism.
It seems to him, as it did to Spinoza, to degrade God to
formulate His attributes. Even His goodness, His wisdom
seem to him a limitation of His absolute amplitude and comprehensive fullness. Revelation strikes him as objectionable
without distinction of its quality: the really oppressive an-
thropomorphic conception of God like the pagan's, as much
as the Epiphany of God in the sanctity of Christ which *per
eminentiam* contains everything. He hates dogma and every
dogmatic religion; the mystery of the Incarnation is to him
the scandal of scandals. . He fails to understand the divine
Beauty shining in the face of Christ, this quite definite, quite
concretely formulated sanctity, which represents not a synthesis of opposites, not a combination of contrary qualities,
but a totally new quality of the Divine and the Holy, coming
from above. He misunderstands the fact that Christ is the
last word of the Cosmos, in whom, despite all concreteness
and definition, all other values are contained *per eminentiam*.

In art this type shows a similar resentment against all
perfection, against all clear formulation. It seems to him flat
and limited. He sees amplitude and infinity only in the endless vista of problems, in things which are unsolved and un-
defined. He finds depth and width only in the tension between
the desire of the artist and his capacity to execute it, in frag-
mentary results. He fails to understand that true amplitude
is comprised in the very quality of value, that infinitude is
the more perfectly expressed, the more completely and perfectly a work of art is realized, like the dying slave of Michel-
angelo or the Ninth Symphony of Beethoven. In life he will

shy at every limitation; he will be happy only when getting on to something new. He would like to get up in the morning, as if there had been no yesterday. He lacks continuity. He confuses licence with true freedom and is insensible to the real oppressiveness and limitation of indefiniteness and chaos.

Even, with an increase of this blindness, the very existence of an absolute truth becomes intolerable to him, because it involves a determination and a limitation of arbitrariness and indefiniteness. He misconceives so completely the peculiar nature of truth and its power of deliverance that he detaches the absolute claim of truth from its quality as truth and treats it as if it were the claim of an error. It is a form of metaphysical libertinism, as in that terrible and notorious utterance of Lessing which places the endless search for truth above the possession of truth. In the end this type lapses into a peculiar paradox: preferring formal knowledge and at first finding a refuge in the wide-meshed net of formality, he ultimately recoils even from this clear definiteness, escapes into formlessness and chaos and rebels against every kind of form as narrowing and arresting.

A third generic error is constituted by 'neutralism' or a constitutional formal blindness to value. I mean the type of person who recognizes no values, only purposes or ends; for whom the world is a web of mere purposes. He fails to see that an event, dominated by a purpose, permeated by a teleological end, does not, merely for that reason belong to the class of things significant in themselves, of values *per se*. He reverses the real relation of end and value. He insists that being an end constitutes a value, instead of understanding that, on the contrary, only being a value makes a thing legitimately and significantly into an end. For such a man, the universe is not a Cosmos of values, but merely an arid organization of ends.—This type also misconceives naturally the whole range of emotion. He equates spirit with intellect and will, and puts emotion—all the significant reactions to value like love, enthusiasm, reverence—on a level with merely passive feeling-states, as no more than meaningless sensation. He is faced with the false alternative: on the one side, spirit and intelligence; on the other, the merely organic life, the unilluminated, non-purposive sphere to which he takes emotion also to belong. The result is a false conception of objectivity and adequacy of reaction. He misconceives the fact that, in face of a Universe of values and especially in face of God, the only reaction or answer which is adequate and objective, i.e. corresponding to the object, must also comprise emotion. Values demand an emotional response. If a person remains untouched by the suffering of another, and is moved by the beauty of a great work of art or of nature to nothing but an intellectual statement of fact, he lacks in the highest degree objectivity and adequacy of response. For all true objectivity and adequacy consist precisely in accepting the object and its *ratio* and in meeting its demands. Such a man follows a wrong conception of life, empty of emotion and of yearning, of a drabness which in no way does justice to the true qualities of the world. He accordingly rejects all real emotion and God-intoxication as sentimentality or subjective bombast. He cherishes a false ideal of reality; only what subserves a temporary end seems to him real and genuine.

Here lies also the root of a false conception of science, namely of the mistaken idea that an attitude which keeps things at a distance and does not allow itself to be touched by them or their world is the only 'objective' and 'scientific' attitude. It is not only Christ who remains unintelligible to this attitude; whole stretches of the world of even natural things are shut out from our minds, if we regard them merely passively from outside, instead of going out to meet them with the reverence due to them. This neutralism ends in a drab ideal of knowledge, for it fears to be biased as soon as it begins to be moved or carried along by the object in question, in other words as soon as a real contact with it is made. In ethics this deformation of knowledge produces Utilitarianism; in the Theory of Knowledge Pragmatism; in life the attitude of the Boeotian and materialist; in art the ideal of the 'New Objectivity'. It is also partly responsible for Bolshevism. The Cosmos, illuminated as it is by value, demands an emotional response; in its degradation to a mere network of ends lies one of the deepest roots of the Bolshevist attitude.

We are now in a position to understand the profound deformations of knowledge which may occur in various types of mind, and the connexion between such types, as well as the generic form of man on the one side, and his capacity of knowledge on the other, and the deeper dependence of knowledge on the fundamental attitude.

A more careful analysis has shown us that, in order to attain to a knowledge which is to be 'unprejudiced', i.e. purely objective, determined by the object and not by our wishes and prejudices, it is not sufficient merely to abstain consciously from all presuppositions concerning the object. Such knowledge demands further the right attitude of the person in order to secure for knowledge a 'clear run', freedom from dimming interferences. But here it becomes evident that the 'objectivity' of the modern university is more appearance than fact. It is a self-delusion: because people are not *consciously* aware of prejudices as such, they imagine that *therefore* their knowledge is free, and that there are no other impediments, outside the sphere of knowledge perhaps, but nevertheless prejudging the result. We cannot remain satisfied with such a merely negative 'absence of prejudice'; we demand more, namely the positively unhampered and free exercise of knowledge which only the right fundamental attitude can guarantee.

In saying this, I do not mean to depreciate the great and

notable body of knowledge which has been the conquest of
the modern university. The achievements in natural science,
history, philology, medicine, law, are in many respects admirable and praiseworthy. At the same time, many have been
the one-sided and erroneous results which have sprung from
that same soil, like Darwinism, Historism, &c. Above all, it
becomes intelligible how precisely in the sphere of Philosophy, despite the utmost intelligence, industry, and erudition, unheard-of platitudes and the most arrant nonsense have
been dished up with solemn scientific pretensions, like
Materialism, Relativism, Scepticism, Positivism, the mecha-
nistic Association-Psychology and many other theories. Not
infrequently the fundamental attitude has obscured knowledge to such an extent that, in spite of unquestionable intelligence, plainly silly assertions have been propounded.

   If we now raise the question, of what kind is the specifically
Catholic attitude to the world of reality, i.e. the attitude
created by Catholic dogma in a person who lives in a world
such as is opened to us by Revelation and represented in the
community of the Church, the answer is that it is precisely
the fundamental attitude which 'delivers' our knowledge,
clears away all the fetters and hindrances to knowledge and
so produces the type of mind capable of doing justice to the
depth and range of reality. The Catholic attitude is specifically soaring, specifically anti-pedantic, anti-self-complacent,
open-minded, filled with respect for reality. The Catholic
conception of the world is such that any one who fixes his
glance upon it and surrenders himself to it must necessarily
possess this soaring, this yearning, open, and reverent mind.
The Catholic world is a Cosmos, ruled by an all-good, all-
powerful, omniscient God who has created all, for whom all
exists, who comprises all in infinite love, who has united us
by and in Christ with Himself supernaturally and has implanted in us His own divine life with baptism, and has

called us to sanctity and eternal beatitude with Himself; has given us the possibility through and by and with Christ to worship Him and sacrifice to Him adequately, and has united us among ourselves in a supernatural communion of Love, communion of merits and prayers. Can we conceive anything more patently antithetical to a mediocre, smug diminutive picture of the world or the commonplace ideal of the 'new Objectivity' of a world without values?

The true Catholic is, to quote again St. Bonaventura, 'a man of desire like Daniel', and the true Catholic attitude is one of humility, free from all resentment, ready to submit and to serve; it is metaphysically courageous, healthy, un-disgruntled, *believing*. I say this is the *Catholic attitude, not* the attitude of the average Catholic. We may indeed be told, not without justification, that many Catholic men of science and erudition show a lack of this attitude more than many non-Catholics. If we think of some of the great men of antiquity, Socrates, Plato, Aristotle, or those of modern times, like Kepler, Newton, Robert Mayer, Leibniz, Humboldt, &c., we find that they were in their fundamental attitude far more 'Catholic' than many a Catholic. How much smugness and pedantry, how much metaphysical indolence do we not find among Catholics and Catholic thinkers and men of science! Certainly; but not *because* they are Catholics; rather because they are *not Catholic enough*, because their attitude has not been formed by Dogma, because Dogma has not become a principle of their life, so that the attitude they display does not fully correspond with what they affirm in their Faith. Where, on the contrary, this is the case, as with St. Augustine, St. Anselm, St. Bonaventura, St. Albertus Magnus, St. Thomas, Pascal, P. Gratry, Cardinal Newman, or Giambattista Rossi, Vico, Toniolo, Dom Germain Morin—there we also find that fundamental attitude which delivers knowledge and opens the way for it.

There is a wide difference between a Catholic scientist or thinker and a scientist and thinker who is incidentally also a Catholic. A large number of Catholic men of science have allowed the modern university to force on them the ideal of its pseudo-freedom from prejudice. They think that they must forget that they are Catholics as soon as they take up their science, in order to work without bias in their research. They surrender thereby the tremendous start which they possess as Catholics in the way of genuine freedom, and assume in its stead an attitude impeding and darkening their outlook. I naturally presuppose a *material* freedom from prejudice and a clear distinction between the *lumen naturale*, natural knowledge, and the *lumen supranaturale* of Revelation. The Catholic thinker, pursuing natural studies, must sharply distinguish between what he knows by Revelation and what is accessible to natural reason. But neither should he forget what he knows by Revelation, for, if Revelation and natural reason represent two distinct paths to truth, there is yet objectively but *one* Truth, which cannot be self-contradictory. If a contradiction results between revealed truth and that yielded by natural reason, the Catholic will, of course, consider such contradiction as merely apparent, since he is convinced that the *lumen naturale*, which after all is also from God, cannot, provided it is allowed to shine without hindrance, lead to a contradiction with the *lumen supranaturale*. He will trust the *lumen supranaturale*. But he will not rush into the assertion that his natural knowledge demonstrates something which in fact it has not yet proved; he will continue his research, go more deeply into it, check everything all the more critically, until the apparent contradiction is solved. Cardinal Newman said:

'(The Catholic) is sure, and nothing shall make him doubt, that if anything seems to be proved by astronomer, or geologist, or chronologist, or antiquarian, or ethnologist, in contradiction to the dogmas of faith, that point will eventually turn out, first, *not* to be proved, or secondly, not *contradictory*, or thirdly, not contradictory to any thing *really* revealed, but to something which has been confused with revelation.'[1]

What a warning against all superficial study this affirmation contains! What a salutary discipline, to go into things and get down to the bedrock of problems! What an incitement, instead of losing ourselves in one-sidedness, with our glance fixed on one single point of the Universe, never to lose sight of the place which our special field of study, however much we cultivate it, occupies within the general structure of reality! What a help to attain to the real *universitas* in the midst of all the errors of one-sided specialization! By all means let us appreciate the autonomous character of a special field; but it is an essential part of its very autonomy that it should occupy this particular place *in the whole*. The Catholic attitude will protect the researcher more than anything else against impatient, pedantic violations of the peculiar and autonomous nature of his special subject, and his reverent listening will prevent him from rushing into hasty systematizations. On the other hand, we can understand how easily a science, and especially a philosophy, resulting from knowledge dimmed or deformed by a false attitude, lapses into contradictions with the content of Dogma, or rather with the natural truths which are implicitly presupposed by Dogma, and then gives rise to Materialism, Psychologism, Relativism, Scepticism, Idealism, Darwinism, &c. But this is not a contradiction which results from knowledge having been given free course, without prejudice, without dogmatic hindrance, but is due rather to the fact that a genuinely unprejudiced, really objective knowledge was never reached, for it was impeded by a false attitude and never really made contact with things.

[1] *Idea of a University* (Christianity and Scientific Investigation), pp. 466–7, Longmans, Green & Co., 1923.

I hope that what I have said will not be misunderstood in the sense that all that is needed to reach adequate and valuable results in knowledge is to possess the right attitude. This is but one, even though a fundamental, pre-requisite. Natural gifts and intelligence are of course also needed, both general intelligence and that particular kind specially required for special fields of knowledge. Such gifts are a gift of God, and being a Catholic is no guarantee of their possession. The utmost piety is no substitute for such talents, and nothing could be more foolish than a sense of superiority in this respect on the part of a Catholic. Neither will the right fundamental attitude dispense the Catholic from the full burden of methodical work, devoted thoroughness and patient, critical application to research. Nor is he dispensed from consulting the results of non-Catholic work, or from appreciating and applying whatever has been obtained by it. All I mean here is that the right fundamental attitude is an essential and decisive factor; and that moreover without it, no adequate knowledge is possible, however much other advantages of intelligence, industry, and thoroughness may be present.

For this reason the Catholic may never artificially divest himself, even in the use of his natural reason, of the attitude which the *lumen supranaturale* imparts to him; on the contrary, for the sake precisely of really unprejudiced, objective knowledge and genuinely scientific work, the Catholic cannot follow too much the guiding influence of Revelation in the formation of his fundamental attitude, cannot be too Catholic. *Catholic Universities* are therefore necessary for the sake of truly adequate objective knowledge, not by any means merely for the protection of the religious convictions of the students. They are needed as the institutions where Catholic thinkers and men of science, supported by a truly Catholic environment, informed in their attitude by the spirit of Christ and of His Church, shall be enabled by a really unbiased, truly liberated and enlightened intelligence to penetrate adequately to reality and to achieve by organized team-work that *universitas* which is nowadays so urgently needed. They must further be institutions in which young people may be educated to that attitude which represents an inevitable pre-requisite for the learner also. A Catholic university would have no meaning, if it were nothing but a collection of Catholic men of thought and science, while following the model of the modern university in its general atmosphere. It requires the conscious production of an atmosphere filled by Christ, an environment imbued with prayer; as an organism it must in its structure and in the common life of its teachers among each other and with their students be thoroughly Catholic. The students must breathe a Catholic air and Catholic spirit which will make them into anti-pedantic, humble, faithful, metaphysically courageous men of winged intelligence and yearning, and therewith capable of truly adequate and objective knowledge. The demand for a Catholic university must therefore be pressed in the name of such adequate knowledge and not by any means only in the interest of 'Catholics'. It does not follow that Catholics should abandon the present universities to their fate and that all Catholic teachers and students should be concentrated in Catholic universities alone. It is rather with the help of Catholic universities, as the homes of a really liberating attitude, that the baneful spell of the pseudo-freedom from prejudice may be broken which hypnotizes non-Catholic universities and fetters Catholic teachers therein. Only through the existence of Catholic universities can the labours of Catholic research in the other universities be brought to full fruition. Catholic universities must create the atmosphere in which the Catholic teacher can find his way back to a true ideal of science and become conscious of the advantage for adequate knowledge which he enjoys through revelation, and of the responsibility of giving to mankind in the way of knowledge what by reason of this advantage he is capable of giving to it. Similarly, the demand for Catholic universities does not imply that Catholics should not frequent non-Catholic universities. If the Catholic student has the material possibility of going to a Catholic university, he will prefer it to a non-Catholic institution, although even then nothing stands in the way of his studying temporarily there also, especially if his subject makes it desirable. But in the absence of the material possibility of frequenting a Catholic university, he will go, as hitherto, to a non-Catholic place of study: he will, however, find even there the spirit of the Catholic university in the instruction of Catholic teachers who have set themselves free from the illusions of a pseudo-freedom from prejudice. Finally, the effect of the Catholic university is not meant to be limited to Catholics only. The liberation of knowledge by an attitude of freedom, humility, and courage will grip also the non-Catholic man of science and thus help to regenerate the spirit of the other universities as well. The Catholic university is not intended as a sort of 'ghetto' for Catholics, but as the nursery of this liberating attitude and the fortress of adequate knowledge, of that attitude which must permeate like a leaven all truly scientific knowledge and study.

. . . .

I turn in conclusion to another aspect of the Catholic university, namely to the features it should present as a community of students and teachers. The function of the student in the university is naturally that of receptivity and of the acquisition of knowledge. If nowadays the demand is often made that students should have more influence on the shaping of the university, that they should be treated less like pupils, that lectures should be replaced by co-operation in study, a Catholic university must insist on the willingness of the student really to learn and to accept instruction. The years of study must after all be a period of growth, of absorption, and the real work must consist in the assimilation of what the student is taught.

Per contra, a Catholic university will display nothing of that professorial superiority which removes the teacher to an Olympian distance from the student. The teacher too must be possessed of that humble attitude which alone enables him to discharge the high and responsible office of searching for and proclaiming the truth. He must stand towards the student, not in a position of schoolmasterly superiority, but of affectionate guidance, informed by a sense of fellowship springing from the bond of service to God in the pursuit of truth.

For the Catholic university must neither as a whole nor in its separate faculties be torn from the context of the whole of human destiny, nor must it become a place for the idolizing of Science or for that modern heresy, the idolatry of the profession. It should rather as a whole bear witness to the true hierarchy of values, a principle which must dominate its smallest details. It must not prefer the absurd claim to be the focal point of the world; its teachers must not present the ridiculous figure of the typical 'professor', who considers the university as his 'world' and, absorbed in his speciality, forgets to be a man, whose true destiny is to know and love God. The Catholic university as a whole must occupy its place in the Cosmos of God and must not pretend to any other position than that which belongs to it in God's plan. Even though devoted wholly to knowledge, it must be inspired by the function and the real end of humanity, which is to glorify God by the sanctification of every man. It must be an institution whose atmosphere is impregnated by Christ and the whole wealth of values, so that the student, however much advance in a special field of study may be his task in the university, yet remains free from the modern professional heresy which places man's centre of gravity no longer in his love of God and his neighbour, but in his achievement in a definite profession, in which his person ranks lower than his achievement. The university must accordingly be a place in which, alongside of specialized studies, the true hierarchy of values is so cultivated as to be a fortress against infection by all those heresies, by all those idols and fetishes which at times poison the air of a period, as nowadays for instance Nationalism, Statolatry, the idolization of mere animal life, and above all that divinization of achievement which stifles all deeper life, replaces virtue by efficiency, has nothing but recreation and amusement to set over against work, leaves no room for contemplation and meditation, makes man into a spiritual cripple and life into a perpetual escape from oneself, which is at bottom nothing but a flight from God.

No less must the university be the place where man never forgets that his primary function is to bring to full fruition that divine life which has been implanted in him by baptism, to imitate Christ, to radiate Christ. For, as stated at the beginning, knowledge will develop free and clear and penetrate the depth of things only in proportion as it is backed by the right attitude; but the right attitude means the full and complete man, open and responsive to the world of values, who lives *in conspectu Dei*, who, to use the words of St. John, lives because he loves. The words of Leonardo da Vinci, 'The greater the man, the deeper his love', must not be forgotten in the university.

For that reason the Catholic university must insist on the transmission not only of specialized knowledge, but also of true general culture, and especially allow no student to leave its walls without a thorough religious education. For not even the most ardent devotion to one's profession can ever nullify the words of Christ: 'Martha, Martha, thou art careful and troubled about many things; but one thing is needful.'

Let us not delude ourselves with the belief that we can ever love a good with greater love than by leaving it in that place where it stands in the eyes of God. To love God more than all else, means also to embrace each good in the deepest and truest love; only in proportion as we love God above all else and see everything *in conspectu Dei*, can we even become capable of full, ardent love. The idolater loves the State, the Nation, Science, Art, not more but less than he who is free from idolatry.

A spirit of freedom, such as only a life from and with Christ can give, must inspire the whole university and blow away all pedantry and caste-spirit and tin-god service. The form of its life must be given not by an academic bureaucracy but by the spirit of Christ and the universal spirit of Catholicism. This alone is right and appropriate for a place devoted to the search for and proclamation of truth. Away with the ideal of pseudo-objectivity, with the secularized atmosphere in which the name of Christ appears like an anachronism! Away with the false conception that man is the more capable of scientific study, the more sterile he is as man, the smaller his living contact is with the whole wealth of the world! Away with the fallacy that a pedantic, distanced neutrality is the true index of the scientific mind! Whatever a university achieves, can be but a part of life as a whole. Knowledge, however great its value *per se*, must as a whole form an organic part of the destiny of the individual and of mankind.

The Catholic university means to give these matters their rightful place. It must be inspired by the spirit of Him to whom all our life, our intellect, our will, our love belong: *Christus heri, hodie et in saecula.*